CW00493752

Tell Them

120 Reasons Why You Must Be a Soul Winner

Dag Heward-Mills

Parchment House

Unless otherwise stated, all Scripture quotations are taken from
the King James Version of the Bible.

TELL THEM

Excerpts in Chapter 1 pages 44, 57, 62, 63, 68 from:
The Final Frontier by Richard Kent and Val Fotherby. Used by permission.
www.finalfrontier.org.uk

Copyright © 2008 Dag Heward-Mills

First published by Lux Verbi.BM (Pty) Ltd. 2008

Published by Parchment House 2011
16th printing 2019

[77]Find out more about Dag Heward-Mills at:

Healing Jesus Campaign
Write to: evangelist@daghewardmills.org
Website: www.daghewardmills.org
Facebook: Dag Heward-Mills
Twitter: @EvangelistDag

ISBN: 978-9988-8505-3-1

Dedication
To
Jimmy and Anita Blavo
Thank you for a great work done in Basel, Switzerland. You have paid the
price to become missionaries to a nation that sent many missionaries to Ghana

All rights reserved under international copyright law. Written permission
must be secured from the publisher to use or reproduce any part of this book.

Contents

Introduction

Soul winning is the all-important job of bringing unsaved people to the Lord Jesus Christ.

Soul winning can be accomplished through personal evangelism, crusades, Christian literature, missionary work, breakfast meetings, Gospel festivals, Christian music, among others.

The oldest method of winning the lost has been through the sacrificing of the lives of missionaries who gave themselves for the salvation of entire nations, tribes and peoples.

Another common method of winning souls is through mass crusades and evangelism through person to person witnessing.

This book is about winning souls in any way possible. It is about personal evangelism, it is about massive crusades, it is about books, it is about missionaries. By all means we must save some!

You may ask, "Why so many reasons?"

Dear friend, I have only given you one hundred and twenty reasons why you must win souls and I can assure you there are many more reasons that I have not been able to share.

Read them and believe them and catch the spirit of Christ, which is the spirit of the soul winner.

CHAPTER 1

One Hundred and Twenty Reasons Why You Must Be a Soul Winner

1. You must be a soul winner because that is the great commission, great command, great mandate, great instruction, great order given to us by our Lord and Saviour Jesus Christ.

   And Jesus came and spake unto them, saying, All power is given unto me in heaven and in earth. Go ye therefore, and teach all nations, baptizing them in the name of the Father, and of the Son, and of the Holy Ghost: Teaching them to observe all things whatsoever I have commanded you: and, lo, I am with you alway, even unto the end of the world. Amen.

   Matthew 28:18-20

2. You must be a soul winner because we are all called to this great work of soul winning.

   For many are called, but few are chosen.

   Matthew 22:14

So the last shall be first, and the first last: for many be called, but few chosen.

Matthew 20:16

What William Booth Said about **the Call**

"Not called! Did you say? *Not heard the call,* I think you should say.

Put your ear down to the Bible, and hear Him bid you go and pull sinners out of the fire of sin! Put your ear down to the burdened, agonized heart of humanity and listen to its pitiful wail for help!

Go stand by the gates of hell, and hear the damned entreat you go to their father's house and bid their brothers and sisters and servants and masters not to come there!

Then look Christ in the face - whose mercy you have professed to obey - and tell Him whether you will join heart and soul and body and circumstances in the march to publish His mercy to the world."

William Booth, *the founder of Salvation Army*

"I believe that in each generation God has called enough men and women to evangelize all the yet unreached tribes of the earth. It is not God who does not call, it is man who will not respond."
Isobel Kuhn, *missionary to China and Thailand*

3. **You must be a soul winner because you were created to carry out the good work of soul winning.**

    For we are his workmanship, CREATED in Christ Jesus UNTO GOOD WORKS, which God hath before ordained that we should walk in them.

    Ephesians 2:10

I once had a chat with a taxi driver in London. I told him I was a Christian, and began to share Christ with him. I also told him about the reality of Heaven and Hell. He laughed and asked whether I really believed in what I was saying.

He said, "If Heaven is real, why don't Christians just kill themselves and move on to Heaven?"

What he was trying to say was that since Heaven is such a nice place, and Christians have nothing to do on earth, they should transfer themselves immediately to Heaven.

If indeed, there is nothing for Christians to do on earth, then this man has a good point. However, the reality is that Christians have a lot to do on earth before getting to Heaven. We are supposed to witness and preach the Gospel of Jesus Christ. We must win the lost at any cost.

The salvation of millions of people depends on us. I'm sorry to say that most Christians have not found out the reasons for which they were saved.

The Bible says that we were saved for a reason - for good works!

> **For we are his workmanship, CREATED in Christ Jesus UNTO GOOD WORKS, which God hath before ordained that we should walk in them.**
>
> **Ephesians 2:10**

Christians are backsliding everyday because they have no purpose for being in the church. People attend church, but after a while they drop out, finding no meaning to church life. Anyone who engages in soul winning will begin to discover the reason for his salvation. Soul winning increases the self-esteem of the Christian.

4. **You must be a soul winner because soul winning gives great joy and energizes Christians.**

> **After these things the Lord appointed other seventy also, and sent them two and two before his face into every city and place...Therefore said he unto them,**

The harvest truly is great...Go your ways: behold, I send you forth...
And the seventy RETURNED AGAIN WITH JOY...

Luke 10:1-3,17

Anytime you go out there preaching you will return with joy. There is joy when souls are won. I cannot explain it. Only a mother can explain how she feels after her baby is born. I have seen many women struggling in labour, but neither pain nor the struggle is able to keep them from rejoicing.

When you bring people to the Lord, you will discover what it means to have the joy of the Lord. I cannot explain it to you. You have to discover it for yourself. I have discovered that my church members become energized when they get involved in soul winning. Soul winning releases the joy of the Lord in the church.

5. **You must be a soul winner because the true greatness of any church is not how many it seats but how many it sends.**

6. **You must be a soul winner because soul winning is the heartbeat of Jesus.**

Some years ago, I had a vision. In this vision, I saw a human heart covered with blood. The heart was beating. God impressed upon my heart that day that the heart cry of Jesus Christ is harvesting the fields. Jesus did not leave His throne for nothing! He came into this world to save sinners.

For the Son of man is come to seek and to save that which was lost.

Luke 19:10

7. **You must be a soul winner because soul winning prevents church splits.**

When your church members are engaged in fruitful activities, they have no time for petty quarrels that bring divisions. *Pastors must teach their church members that a soul is a soul, and is precious to God.*

When church members are conscious of the souls that need to be won, their priorities become biblical priorities.

Church splits and divisions are avoided. When too many Christians are in one place doing nothing, it often generates hurts, quarrels and wounds.

8. You must be a soul winner because soul winning generates divine support and protection.

> *"It is not in our choice to spread the gospel or not. It is our death if we do not."*
> **Peter Taylor Forsyth**

When you win souls, you generate divine support for all that you are doing.

As you read the Bible, you will discover that soul winning generates heavenly joy. There is a heavenly response to each and every soul won for the Lord.

> **I say unto you, that likewise JOY SHALL BE IN HEAVEN over one sinner that repenteth, more than over ninety and nine just persons, which need no repentance.**
> **Likewise, I say unto you, there is JOY IN THE PRESENCE OF THE ANGELS OF GOD over one sinner that repenteth.**
> **Luke 15:7,10**

Churches must know why they exist: to generate souls for Heaven. Embassies exist to represent the government from which they came. Similarly, churches are heavenly embassies.

Many pray that God will keep them from evil. Did you know that divine protection is made available for all who take part in doing God's will?

Psalm 91 says that, God will keep and protect you because you have set your love on Him.

> **Because he hath set his love upon me, therefore WILL I DELIVER HIM: I will set him on high, because he hath known my name. He shall call upon me, and I will answer him: I WILL BE WITH HIM IN TROUBLE; I WILL DELIVER HIM, and honour him. With long life will I satisfy him, and shew him my salvation.**
>
> **Psalm 91:14-16**

When you set your love on God to please Him, God says that He will deliver you. I believe that I am doing the will of God. Perhaps that is the only reason why I am still alive. Just like Paul, I have had a few near-death experiences, including near plane crashes and car accidents.

> **Are they ministers of Christ? (I speak as a fool) I am more; in labours more abundant, in stripes above measure, in prisons more frequent, in deaths oft.**
> **Of the Jews five times received I forty stripes save one. Thrice was I beaten with rods, once was I stoned, thrice I suffered shipwreck, a night and a day I have been in the deep;**
>
> **2 Corinthians 11:23-25**

In all these things I can speak like Paul and say that God delivered me from them all.

> **For I am persuaded, that neither death, nor life, nor angels, nor principalities, nor powers, nor things present, nor things to come, Nor height, nor depth, nor any other creature, shall be able to separate us from the love of God, which is in Christ Jesus our Lord.**
>
> **Romans 8:38-39**

I see God delivering you now! I see God helping you in your time of trouble! I see God standing with you because you have set your love on Him!

Do you want to stay in the will of God? Do you want your church to grow? Be a soul winner today. You will see a difference in the church.

I only see my pastoral job fulfilled when I am able to convert a member into a minister. I want every member of my church to be a soul winner. I want them to have fruit to show one day. If there is no harvesting of souls, there will be no sheep for the pastor to look after. Every pastor can do the work of an evangelist!

9. **You must be a soul winner because soul winning prevents you from polishing the same coins over and over.**

> **Either what woman having ten pieces of silver, if she lose one piece, doth not light a candle, and sweep the house, and seek diligently till she find it?**
> **And when she hath found it, she calleth her friends and her neighbours together, saying, Rejoice with me; for I have found the piece which I had lost.**
> **Likewise, I say unto you, there is joy in the presence of the angels of God over one sinner that repenteth.**
> **Luke 15:8-10**

It is important to avoid the mistake of carefully counting and polishing over and over our treasured coins instead of going to look for the lost coin - which is the unbeliever.

Why is it that only a few people get involved in soul winning? When people start new churches, we do not see much soul winning. It is easier to start a church by "stealing" sheep than by winning souls, because it is easier to destroy than to build!

Before Jesus went away, He emphasized the preaching of the Gospel to the lost. It is sad to note that, winning the lost has now become a side issue in the Church. Although the command to go out and reach the lost was a priority, it has been relegated to the background.

Many of us are making the mistake of "polishing the same coins" repeatedly. The already established church members are the nine coins you will read about in the passage below. Ministers spend most of the time polishing these nine coins over and over again!

> **Either what woman having ten pieces of silver, if she lose one piece, doth not light a candle, and sweep the house, and seek diligently till she find it?**
> **And when she hath found it, she calleth her friends and her neighbours together, saying, REJOICE WITH ME; FOR I HAVE FOUND THE PIECE WHICH I HAD LOST.**
>
> **Luke 15:8-9**

The lost coin represents lost and dying sinners. Sometimes when I minister in a church, I look at the crowd and think to myself, that these are the nine coins I'm going to polish again!

We bring in anointed teachers and spectacular prophets to polish our coins. We hold marriage seminars to polish the coins. More polishing! We have home cell meetings and do more polishing. The polishing goes on! We have end of year get-togethers for our nice Christian brothers and sisters. More polishing! All this while, the one coin is changing colour in the corner. The unbelievers are getting more and more hardened as we concentrate on ourselves.

It is time for us to turn our attention to the supreme task of the Church: win the lost at any cost! It is time for us to harvest the masses that are waiting for a preacher. **We must avoid the mistake of polishing, followed by more polishing, followed by even more polishing of the same coin.**

Every Christian is first a soul winner. Thank God for the gifts of drama and singing, but you must first be a witness. After you are a soul winner, you may then go on to be a teacher, shepherd, musician, singer or administrator.

Christians who become singers without being soul winners do not understand why they sing. They often think that they are supposed to impress people with their nice songs.

You are a Christian singer and not a singing Christian - there is a difference!

Whatever we find ourselves doing in the body of Christ, let us know that we are first expected to bring souls to the Lord.

10 . **We must be soul winners because we must save people from building their houses on the sand.**

> **And every one that heareth these sayings of mine, and doeth them not, shall be likened unto a foolish man, which built his house upon the sand:**
> **And the rain descended, and the floods came, and the winds blew, and beat upon that house; and it fell: and great was the fall of it.**
>
> **Matthew 7:26-27**

> **Except the LORD build the house, they labour in vain that build it: except the LORD keep the city, the watchman waketh but in vain.**
>
> **Psalms 127:1**

11. **You must be a soul winner because soul winning helps you to avoid a false balance.**

> **A false balance is abomination to the Lord...**
>
> **Proverbs 11:1**

I see an imbalance in the work of the Lord. A false balance is a terrible thing. The Bible calls an imbalance an abomination. Too much emphasis is placed on the already established church, to the neglect of a lost and dying world.

It is like ten people trying to lift up a heavy log. Nine of them are at one end of the log and only one person is at the other end. This is an imbalance.

Alarming Statistics

Some statistics tell us that there are over one thousand groups (tribes and races) of people, who have never heard the Gospel even once. It is also said that ninety-four per cent of ministers are preaching to nine per cent of the world's population.

What does this mean? It means that six per cent of all ministers are struggling with the remaining ninety-one per cent of the world's harvest! It is no wonder that religions like Islam are gaining grounds in large sections of the world.

Many Died as Soul Winners

How many anointed Charismatic pastors would opt to go to remote parts of any country? After visiting the north of Ghana, I realized that many people live in abject poverty. I realized how difficult it must have been for any missionary, Ghanaian or otherwise, to live there!

Today, people are no longer willing to make great sacrifices for the expansion of the Gospel.

Dear friend, we need to remember that people laid down their lives for the establishment of the Church. I appreciate the Swiss, German and Scottish missionaries who came to Ghana many years ago and established the Church. Many of them died of malaria. They would send back messages saying that all the missionaries sent were dead. The churches in Europe would respond by sending more missionaries.

Many missionaries died and others, such as Rev. F.A. Ramseyer (1868-1869), were captured and taken to Kumasi by Ashanti invaders.

Many of these missionaries such as Johannes Christaller achieved remarkable milestones, such as the Twi (a local Ghanaian language) translation of the Bible, Twi Grammar, a collection of 3,600 Twi proverbs and Twi translations of Christian doctrinal works.

Johannes Zimmerman, founded the Basel Mission Schools at Osu and Abokobi (1854). He also made notable translations into the Ga language (another local dialect).

All of this means that, European men of God laid down their lives in Ghana for the establishment of the Church. They did it at a time when there were no airplanes, electricity, running water, cars, televisions and telephones. Even now, with many of these comforts readily available, people are not prepared to go on similar sacrificial missionary journeys.

These apostles came, knowing that their predecessors had died or had been captured and killed. You may curse the White man for the slave trade; however, there were some genuine apostles who brought the Gospel to us in Africa. They learnt our language! They translated the Bible for us! They lived and died amongst a strange people! All this for the love of Christ!

Where is this sacrificial love for the Gospel and for our Lord? I have the feeling that Heaven will reveal a host of unknown heroes. The people we hail today as great men of God may not be the ones to receive the laurels on "prize-giving day" in Heaven!

If we in our own country are not prepared to lay down our lives for this Gospel, the Church is not going to expand! It is time for us to send people out to remote towns and villages where Christ is not known. It is time for us to return to the days of true missionaries. It is time for pastors to decide whether they are called, or whether they are just looking for another job avenue.

I Saw the Graves of White Apostles

I remember attending a funeral in the Akwapim Mountains of Ghana. Whilst at the cemetery, waiting for the burial service to start, I decided to take a stroll through the graveyard. I read the names on some of the tombs. Initially, I thought I would only see the names of the local Akwapim people. But I was surprised to find the names of Swiss and German people on some of the tombstones. I realized that I was looking at the names of Swiss missionaries who had died on those mountains a hundred years ago. It struck me that these people had paid a great price for the Church to expand to Ghana.

Today, if I do an altar call asking for missionaries to go to certain remote places, I will get little or no response. However, if I do an altar call for missionaries to go to New York or Paris, I will have a huge response. What is happening? Do we really care about the lost, or are we only concerned about becoming affluent and popular pastors in big cities?

An Alternative Source of Employment?

I often wonder what people mean when they say they are called to the ministry. Many people take full-time ministry as an alternative source of employment. I am NOT in full-time ministry because I have no other job. I see it as a calling. I see it as something I have to do.

I can confidently say with Paul, "Woe is unto me, if I preach not the Gospel." If I wanted to be rich, I would not be a minister. God blessed me with a very noble and lucrative profession - the medical profession.

Why I Became a Priest

The ministry of the Lord Jesus Christ is a calling and must always remain a calling. One minister was asked, "How did you get into the ministry?"

He answered, "I was never good at anything in school, so I decided to become a priest."

If that is the reason why you became a minister, you are not likely to carry the burden that Jesus carried! You are not likely to transmit the burden of the lost to your congregation.

It is time for us to get back to the primary call of the Church. It is time for us to make soul winning our main task.

Soul winning is the main task of Lighthouse Chapel International. All choristers in my church go on evangelistic outreaches. They win souls and follow them up. I have made them understand that they are Christian singers and not singing Christians! Ushers in my church do "person-to-person" witnessing. At one time, our ushering ministry became very large because the leader of the ushers often took the ushers out on "bus-to-bus" preaching.

Let us analyse the number of harvest fields and the number of workers we have. There is a great imbalance between the harvest fields and the labourers. It is time for us to look at maps and find out where the sinners are and go to them. **It is time for the forgotten ones to hear. It is time for the poor ones to hear**. It is time for the neglected ones to receive some light. It is time for people to graduate from the university and say, "I want to give the rest of my days to the ministry of the Lord Jesus Christ. I want to win the lost at any cost!"

A Mega Crusade

I once organized a crusade in a prominent park in my city. An evangelist had travelled all the way from America to preach at this crusade. When it was about time for the sermon, I decided to do something unusual.

There was a large crowd present. Everyone was seated in great expectation. I thought to myself that almost everybody in that crowd was a Christian. We had advertised the programme on television, and Christians had gathered in their numbers.

I said to the pastors around me, "Let's send these people out to invite sinners to the meeting."

Many of the pastors were unsure of what was happening. I said to them, "The reason for which we are gathered is to win souls for Christ. If there are no lost souls in the crowd, what is the use of this programme? Why did we spend all this money?"

The crowd was sent out and they happily invited hundreds of hungry souls. Some might have thought that at such an international forum, doing something like that was unacceptable. But that night, we reaped a mighty harvest of souls for the Lord.

12. You must be a soul winner and allow the Lord to send you out to win souls so that you will not be sent out by persecution and other troubles, like the early church.

> **And Saul was consenting unto his death. And at that time there was a great persecution against the church which was at Jerusalem; and they were all scattered abroad throughout the regions of Judaea and Samaria, except the apostles. And devout men carried Stephen to his burial, and made great lamentation over him.**
>
> **As for Saul, he made havock of the church, entering into every house, and haling men and women committed them to prison. THEREFORE THEY THAT WERE SCATTERED ABROAD WENT EVERYWHERE PREACHING THE WORD.**
>
>

Acts 8:1-4

> *"To stay here and disobey God - I can't afford to take the consequence. I would rather go and obey God than to stay here and know that I disobeyed."*
>
>

Amanda Berry Smith

God is issuing a warning to the Church: "If you don't spread out, I will spread you out myself." Did you know that the early church did not fully obey the instruction to win souls?

God has different ways of getting us to obey Him. When the early church refused to go out, God allowed a strong persecution to come her way. He sent a man, Saul, to harass the church until the people were forced to travel away from Jerusalem in order to avoid death.

Many churches experience splits and painful divisions. If you look carefully, you will realize that many of these painful divisions actually lead to church growth in the long run. The reason is that more ministers are allowed to develop their gifts and more churches are established. **Are you waiting for your church to split up before you obey God?**

I laugh when people criticize me for planting many churches in the same city. I muse that these people do not know what they are talking about. I have very large and successful branch churches just a few metres from where I am. Most of these pastors used to work with me at the headquarters. When I sensed the potential in them to minister, I sent them out to begin churches. Most of them have succeeded in establishing solid Bible-based churches, and the entire ministry has expanded because of this.

13. You must be a soul winner because soul winning fulfils the principle of gaining by trading.

God has given us His great salvation. He expects us to take this pound of salvation and share it. When we share what He has given us, the gift of God increases. Do you want more anointing on your life? There is a process by which anointing and gifts increase. It is called "gaining by trading".

> **...that he might know how much every man had GAINED BY TRADING.**
> **Luke 19:15**

The more you do God's work, the more the anointing increases. Do not forget the story of the master who gave his servants ten pounds. He told them, "Occupy until I come."

When the master came back, some of the servants had more than others.

> **Then came the first, saying, Lord, THY POUND [anointing] HATH GAINED ten pounds.**
> **Luke 19:16**

The pound represents the anointing. The pound represents the gifts that God has given to you. **That gift supernaturally increases as you begin working!** When you plunge into soul winning and evangelism, the anointing on your life will double and triple. *I see you gaining by trading! I see you gaining a new anointing by trading with what God has given you! I see you preaching to thousands and doing miracles!*

I always enjoy going back to the classroom where I began my ministry. Sometimes, I stand outside the window of the classroom where I began and stare at the few chairs within it. I remember preaching to about ten people.

For years, I have been in the pulpit, preaching every Sunday and Tuesday. At the beginning, I preached to about five people. But I have definitely gained by trading. I now minister to thousands of people every week. I always thank God for His mercy.

14. You must be a soul winner because soul winning earns you the right to kingdom promotion.

After improving through the secret of gaining by trading, God will lift you up by another method I call *"kingdom promotion"*. Gaining by trading makes the pound you have swell up. But when the master assesses that you have gained something by trading, you will receive a "kingdom promotion".

A "kingdom promotion" is an elevation that is so lofty that it makes you marvel at how far the Lord has brought you. The man who was given authority over ten cities could not compare his new status with his former job of trading with ten pounds.

> **...thou hast been faithful in a very little, have thou authority over ten cities.**
>
> **Luke 19:17**

In the day you receive a "kingdom promotion", you will know that God has truly lifted you out of the dust.

15. You must be a soul winner because soul winning will help you avoid a murder charge. You do not want to account for the blood of anyone.

Son of man, I have made thee a watchman unto the house of Israel: therefore hear the word at my mouth, and give them warning from me.

When I say unto the wicked, Thou shalt surely die; and thou givest him not warning, nor speakest to warn the wicked from his wicked way, to save his life; the same wicked man shall die in his iniquity; but his blood will I require at thine hand.

Ezekiel 3:17-18

What does this mean: "Blood will be required at your hand?" I remember when my father, a lawyer, was the attorney for a man accused of murder. My wife Adelaide, and her friend Rev. Sackey, were junior lawyers working with my father. It was an interesting case to follow.

Both the families of the accused and the deceased were present in Court. Before the jury gave its final verdict, Rev. Sackey had to make a final address in defence of the accused man. The packed to capacity courtroom was tense, as both families followed the proceedings. All concerned parties wanted to know whether this man was guilty or not.

What was happening? People were requiring the blood of the slain farmer from the hands of the accused.

When the Bible says that God will require the blood of sinners at your hand, it simply means that you will be asked to answer for a murder charge.

I am sure you don't think of yourself as a murderer or a killer. But by refusing to warn sinners, by refusing to hold crusades and by refusing to do door-to-door witnessing, you are indirectly assigning people to Hell. God says that He will hold you responsible! That is why you must preach the Gospel in every corner, on every highway and on every street.

We must have the attitude that the salvation of the whole world depends on us. Without this attitude, we will always assume that some zealous evangelist will do the job.

Dear friend, there are very few zealous evangelists today. Evangelists have very little support for their work. It seems that it is much more profitable to be a pastor than to be an evangelist. The offerings that are available to the evangelist cannot be compared to the offerings that pastors receive from overfed Christian millionaires who sit on the pews of the church.

Why would anyone want to be an evangelist? It is a truly thankless job and the rewards can only be found in eternity. I believe that God divinely blesses anyone who chooses to win souls and makes it his life's work.

16. You must be a soul winner because it makes you have beautiful feet.

And how shall they preach, except they be sent? as it is written, How beautiful are the feet of them that preach the gospel of peace, and bring glad tidings of good things!

Romans 10:15

How beautiful are the feet of those that preach the Gospel and bring good news! What is good news? Is the good news that electricity has been extended to the village? Is the good news that pipe-borne water is now available in your town? Is the good news that we have a new President? None of these is the good news of the Gospel. **There is no news like the Gospel of Jesus Christ.** It is the only answer to the problems of a lost human race.

The whole world is confused. If one or two cruise missiles were sold, the problems of millions of people could be solved! There is an imbalance in the distribution of wealth. The poor are getting poorer and the rich are getting richer. There seems to be a curse in certain sections of the earth. Many people cannot make ends meet.

In the under-developed world, people talk about the global economic crisis and children not having enough to eat. In the rich western world, people are worried because some won't have turkey and salad to eat at Christmas! Everyone has his or her own problems!

What is the good news that these people need? Everyone needs the Gospel. The Gospel is good for the rich and for the poor. **The Gospel is good news for both western and eastern nations.** The preaching of Jesus Christ has power in the land of the communists as well as in the land of the capitalists.

17. **You must be a soul winner because the emphasis of the end-time Church must be: Win the world and precipitate the second coming of Christ.**

> **For many shall come in my name, saying, I am Christ; and shall deceive many. And ye shall hear of wars and rumours of wars: see that ye be not troubled: for all these things must come to pass, but the end is not yet. For nation shall rise against nation, and kingdom against kingdom: and there shall be famines, and pestilences, and earthquakes, in divers places. All these are the beginning of sorrows.**
> **Then shall they deliver you up to be afflicted, and shall kill you: and ye shall be hated of all nations for my name's sake.**
> **And then shall many be offended, and shall betray one another, and shall hate one another. And many false prophets shall rise, and shall deceive many.**
> **And because iniquity shall abound, the love of many shall wax cold.**
> **But he that shall endure unto the end, the same shall be saved.**
> **And this gospel of the kingdom shall be preached in all the world for a witness unto all nations; AND THEN SHALL THE END COME.**
> **Matthew 24:5-14**

I see a last wave of miracle power coming into the earth. It is going to help us to reach out to the harvest fields. God will support us! The power of the Holy Spirit is on us as we set out to tackle the harvest. *Do you know that the rapture will not occur until the Gospel has been preached to all nations?*

Jesus gave us signs of the end. The last and specific sign was the preaching of the Gospel to the nations.

The end of the world depends on your soul winning. Let us arise together and bring about the return of Jesus Christ to rule this world in authority and power.

18. You must be a soul winner because it is the distinctive mark of being a Christian. As James S. Stewart said, "The concern for world evangelization…can never be the province of a few enthusiasts, a sideline or a specialty of those who happen to have a bent that way. It is the distinctive mark of being a Christian."

Harvesting the lost is the first and foremost task of the whole Church. I am talking to prophets. I am talking to teachers. I am talking to singers. I am ministering to administrators. The Gospel is the first thing. We must win the lost at any cost!

And the gospel must FIRST be published among all nations.

Mark 13:10

Let soul winning be our chief task. Let it be the primary focus of every church. That is the Great Commission given to us. When our choirs minister in song, let the lost souls be our target.

Dear prophet, when the Lord uses you to minister in signs and wonders, remember that signs and wonders are to attract *sinners to Christ.* If signs and wonders are just being used to attract rich people to your group, you have not understood why God made you a prophet.

The ministry gifts are not given for you to acquire nice houses and cars. They are power instruments for reaping the harvest. When people come to you with financial and marital problems, please direct them first to Christ. Make sure that they are saved in the Lord.

An elderly man once came to see me. He had a string of problems. He wanted me to pray for his clinic, his marriage and his home. He felt that he needed deliverance, ministration and prayer!

I asked him a simple question, "Are you born again?"

He did not even know what that meant! I knew immediately that this man needed Christ *first*. I immediately led him in the sinner's prayer to receive the Lord. It was only after that, that I considered his other problems.

Dear revivalist, I am very happy about the spectacular display of signs and wonders in your ministry! We have prayed for years that signs and wonders would come back to the Church. But for goodness sake, remember why signs and wonders are being restored to the Church. They are being restored for the harvest. Please use your ability to gather crowds to win souls.

I have watched as large crowds gather in the megachurches of today. It is pathetic to see them gather and disperse time and time again, without a single salvation altar call being made. If we do not do the right thing with our church growth, God will raise up others. We must win the lost at any cost!

19. You must be a soul winner today and overcome the sin of distraction.

But and if that evil servant shall say in his heart, My lord delayeth his coming;
And shall begin to smite his fellowservants, and to eat and drink with the drunken;
The lord of that servant shall come in a day when he looketh not for him, and in an hour that he is not aware of...
Matthew 24:48-50

In the Scripture above, the servant was distracted and began to concern himself with destroying his fellow servants. It is very easy to be distracted from your primary task. The church has become so established that sometimes she loses sight of why she exists. As a full-time minister, I try to stay focused on my calling.

I believe in interaction between churches. However, there are times when those interactions can be distractive. Contrary to traditional belief, it has been shown that a lot of trans-church interaction does not lead to church growth. Hurts, wounds and quarrels have been generated through some of these interactions. Pastors end up spending a lot of time ironing out their differences, and all that time could have been spent fulfilling the primary call.

Our church was once attacked by a mob of individuals brandishing sticks and stones. We had a serious confrontation with them and many people got hurt in the process. The scene was played back on national television and many people got to know about it.

I was surprised, though not shocked, to hear that some Christians said, "It serves them right!" Many people are jealous of their brother's success, and get into conflicts like Cain and Abel did. This is very natural and so I have learnt to stay in my corner and do the work of God. Conflicts and divisions within the church may also distract you from your primary goal of reaching the lost.

If your church is involved in a major internal conflict, I will give you a suggestion. Start outreach immediately! Don't say, "I will wait for the problem to resolve before I embark on evangelism." Embarking on outreaches will help to turn attention away from the problem.

20. You must be a soul winner today and overcome the sin of procrastination.

And Moses said unto Pharaoh, Glory over me: when shall I intreat for thee, and for thy servants, and for thy people, to destroy the frogs from thee and thy houses, that they may remain in the river only?
And he said, tomorrow...

Exodus 8:9-10

Pharaoh could have been set free from the frogs on that very day but he asked that the frogs be taken on the morrow. How strange it is that we put off important things to a later time when we could do them immediately.

The cardinal enemy of all evangelism and outreach is the demon of procrastination. Outreach is often postponed and put off till later. Some people go as far as cancelling their scheduled outreach programmes.

"I will witness to him tomorrow," they say. "We will do a crusade next year; after all, there are other pressing problems to deal with."

Years ago, I learnt something very important from a Full Gospel Businessmen's Fellowship meeting. I was invited to be the main speaker at a breakfast meeting. When I finished ministering, I sat down on stage as they concluded the meeting with some announcements.

One of the announcements struck me and the Lord spoke to me at that moment. They announced that their next outreach was to be held in a month's time.

Right there, the Lord showed me that these people had planned a rigid schedule of monthly outreaches that were not negotiable. They were not negotiable in the sense that they could not be postponed or cancelled. The speakers for their meetings were sometimes scheduled a year in advance. Whether there was a tidal wave, economic upheaval or a political earthquake, the outreach was going to come on.

From that moment, I became convinced that fixing an inflexible monthly outreach for every fellowship and ministry in my church was the way forward.

There are many cares and problems of this life. Many people are struggling to pay school fees, build houses and buy food to eat. Many people have marital problems and do not know how peace is going to come to their homes. They say, "How can I think of evangelism when I have so many problems?"

And the cares of this world...choke the word...

Mark 4:19

Dear Christian friend, do not let the cares of this world choke the call of God on your life. I see you rising up in spite of every weight and difficulty in your life! He that winneth souls is wise! Be wise now! Win a soul today! The soul you bring to the Lord may become a blessing to you in different ways!

...he that winneth souls is wise.

Proverbs 11:30

"No reserves, no regrets, no retreats."

William Borden

21. **You must be a soul winner because that is the reason why Jesus came to the earth.**

    For the Son of man IS COME TO SEEK and to save that which was lost.

    Luke 19:10

22. **Soul winning is important if we want to be Christ-like.**

    How many of us want to be Christ-like? Christ was a soul winner and in order to imitate Him we must be soul winners.

    For the Son of man IS COME TO SEEK and to save that which was lost.

    Luke 19:10

23. **You must be a soul winner because every Christian is basically a "witness" of what he has experienced with Christ.**

    He may be a teacher, shepherd, pastor, writer, singer, prophet, musician, administrator, but he is basically a soul winner.

    But ye shall receive power, after that the Holy Ghost is come upon you: and ye shall be witnesses unto me

both in Jerusalem, and in all Judaea, and in Samaria, and unto the uttermost part of the earth.

Acts 1:8

James S. Stewart said, "The concern for world evangelization is not something tacked onto a man's personal Christianity, which he may take or leave as he chooses. It is rooted in the character of God who has come to us in Christ Jesus. Thus, it can never be the province of a few enthusiasts, a sideline or a specialty of those who happen to have a bent that way. It is the distinctive mark of being a Christian."

J. Stuart Holden said, "'Go ye' is as much a part of Christ's gospel as 'come unto me'. You are not even a Christian until you have honestly faced your responsibility in regard to the carrying of the gospel to the ends of the earth."

24. **You must be a soul winner because the harvest is overwhelmingly gigantic and very few Christians concern themselves with this work.**

    Then saith he unto his disciples, THE HARVEST TRULY IS PLENTEOUS, but the labourers are few;
    Matthew 9:37

25. **Soul winning is important because it proves that you have the heart of the Father, which was moved with compassion for the lost.**

    But when he saw the multitudes, HE WAS MOVED WITH COMPASSION on them, because they fainted, and were scattered abroad, as sheep having no shepherd.
    Matthew 9:36

26. **You must be a soul winner because the divine balance of ministry shows that 20% of all ministry is for evangelism.**

    The Scripture is clear that one out of the five primary ministries of apostles, prophets, pastors, teachers and evangelists is dedicated entirely to the winning of the lost. In our modern ministry, far less than 20% of all ministry is dedicated to evangelism. In reality, almost all ministry is dedicated to pastoring and prophesying to the existing prosperous and overfed sheep.

> **And he gave some, apostles; and some, prophets; and some, evangelists; and some, pastors and teachers;**
> **Ephesians 4:11**

27. You must be a soul winner because over one thousand peoples have not heard the Gospel once. The forgotten ones must hear too.

> **And I saw another angel fly in the midst of heaven, having the everlasting gospel to preach unto them that dwell on the earth, and to every nation, and kindred, and tongue, and people,**
> **Revelation 14:6**

a. If the world had 100 people, 60 of them would be from Asia.

b. If the world had 100 people, 13 of them would be from Africa.

c. If the world had 100 people, 12 of them would be from Europe.

d. If the world had 100 people, 9 of them would be from South America.

e. If the world had 100 people, 5 of them would be from North America.

f. If the world had 100 people, 1 would be from Oceania.

You can see from the above distribution that the emphasis on ministry is on a few prosperous Americans. The large part of the harvest field has fallen into the hands of various religions and cults whilst Christians continue to emphasize on a "crossless" prosperity and non-sacrificial message that weakens our ability to reach the lost. Another interesting statistic is that 94% of all pastors preach to 9% of the world's harvest and 6% of all pastors preach to 91% of the world's harvest.

William Borden said, as he reflected on the numbers of Christian workers in the USA as compared to those among unreached peoples in China, "If 10 men are carrying a log - nine of them on the little end and one at the heavy end - and you want to help, which end will you lift on?"

28. **Soul winning is important to prevent the invasion of false religions into our communities. This is an obvious effect of the absence of soul winning in the church.**

29. **Soul winning is important because they cannot hear or be saved without a preacher.**

   How then shall they call on him in whom they have not believed? and how shall they believe in him of whom they have not heard? and how shall they hear without a preacher?

   Romans 10:14

30. **Soul winning is important now because the night comes when no one can work.**

   One day, Jesus said something prophetic. He said, "I must work while it is day for the night will come when no one can work." No matter how anointed or gifted you are, you will not be able to work at night.

   I must work the works of him that sent me, while it is day: THE NIGHT COMETH, WHEN NO MAN CAN WORK.

   John 9:4

   Jesus spoke of a season when no one would be able to do God's work. He said a time would come when no one would be able to evangelise anymore. Take a look at the global harvest field; you will find that the night has fallen on certain sections of the globe. It is now impossible to harvest the fields in those parts of the world.

   Look at the Islamic nations of the world. There are millions of people under the cloud of strict Islamic rule. Christianity is virtually forbidden in many of these places. It is very dangerous to preach the Gospel in some countries.

Do you remember the days of the Soviet Union? Communism stamped out all true church life. Many Russians died without hearing the Gospel of Jesus Christ because it was technically, legally and physically impossible to preach the Gospel over there.

Look at sections of Africa today. Many African nations are battlefields. I cannot send somebody's husband or father to certain countries in Africa. How would I explain to the wife if the pastor got killed? It is impossible to drive through certain African nations. Rebels have taken over large sections of many countries.

The night has fallen in these places. That is why we need to take advantage of every opportunity. Many people think that peace will always prevail.

Look at countries like Liberia and Zaire, which enjoyed many years of relative peace. Perhaps we did not know that it was daytime in those places. As I am writing this book, there is war in the former Zaire. I cannot go there and I would not like to send anybody there. The night has come when no one can work in Zaire.

In some Western countries like Switzerland, Christians are not permitted to preach on the streets or to hold crusades as freely as we do in Ghana. The police have questioned our Swiss pastor during Gospel concert outreaches. Meanwhile, occult and witchcraft shops are springing up freely all over Switzerland.

Many parts of Europe are hard ground for the Gospel. The spirit of atheism is so entrenched that the preaching of the Gospel now looks absurd.

However, there are many places where the night has not yet fallen. It is easier to preach the Gospel of Jesus Christ in these places. Even in nations where the Gospel is permitted, you will find that some sections of the population are more open to the Gospel.

31. Soul winning is important because it gives vision to a church.

Ministers have a vision when they become soul winners. Businessmen have a vision when they become soul winners. Ordinary Christians have a vision when they become soul winners. Soul winning is the great vision that all churches must have.

> **Where there is no vision, the people perish: but he that keepeth the law, happy is he.**
>
> **Proverbs 29:18**

32. You must be a soul winner because shepherds and pastors are supposed to notice the lost souls around them.

> **But when he saw the multitudes, he was moved with compassion on them, because they fainted, and were scattered abroad, as sheep having no shepherd.**
> **Then saith he unto his disciples, The harvest truly is plenteous, but the labourers are few;**
>
> **Matthew 9:36-37**

I realize that many Christians, and even pastors, do not notice the harvest of souls around them. I see the multitude of people all around and wonder if these people know Christ!

Sometimes, when driving to church, I see crowds of people streaming down the road. I often ask myself, "How many of these people know Christ as their Saviour? How many will really die in Christ? How many of them go to church on Sunday morning?"

Recently, my wife and I drove through the streets of Johannesburg (in South Africa), which is a very beautiful city. We saw many nice buildings. At one point during the ride, we had a good view of the entire city beautifully lit with thousands of lights.

As I looked down, I suddenly thought to myself that there are so many people in the world. South Africa is full of souls. I did not only see the nice buildings, but I saw the vastness of the harvest, which lay virtually untouched.

Dear friend, there are millions of people around you. I don't know if you notice that there are so many precious souls who have just a short time to live before tasting eternity. How many people will die in Christ? How many will live again?

Every pastor's burden must be for souls. The burden for souls is not just for evangelists! The Lord Jesus testified of Himself:

> **I am the good shepherd [pastor]...**
>
> **John 10:11**

A good shepherd means a good pastor. Jesus was the best pastor that ever lived and yet He said:

> **For the Son of man is come to SEEK and to SAVE THAT WHICH WAS LOST.**
>
> **Luke 19:10**

A good pastor is one who seeks and saves the lost. Some people think that a good pastor just thinks about caring for already existing sheep. Do you remember this Scripture?

> **This is a faithful saying, and worthy of all acceptation, that Christ Jesus came into the world to save sinners; of whom I am chief.**
>
> **1 Timothy 1:15**

33. You must be a soul winner because soul winning is the supreme task of every kind of minister, even if they are not evangelists.

God gave the five-fold ministry to the body of Christ to ensure that the work of Christ continues. We have apostles, prophets, evangelists, pastors and teachers. What is the duty of these different ministries? **The ultimate goal for every minister is to win the lost to Christ.**

When you go into the hospital, you will find secretaries, cleaners and even messengers. All of these people working in the hospital, have the ultimate goal of providing health services for the community. Every secretary employed by the hospital should know that the letters she types contribute towards this goal. So it is with pastors, prophets and teachers. Our ultimate goal is to reap the harvest. When we forget the main reason for which the church exists, we begin to go into error.

Sometimes when you talk to pastors, you cannot help but realize that soul winning is one of the last things on their minds. How do I know that many ministers do not care about souls anymore? By listening to what they preach and watching how church services are conducted. Many ministers hold services without making an altar call for the lost. This goes to show that the salvation of the lost is not a burden on their hearts, for "out of the abundance of the heart the mouth speaks". **When I see a large crowd, what occurs to me is the souls that can be saved.** After an impressive power display, what about the souls who are lost? I can see the harvest. I can see the whitened and ripened harvest fields virtually untouched.

Elections Expose the Harvest Fields

In 1996, presidential and parliamentary elections were held in Ghana. Out of the various political parties contesting, there were two main contenders. After voting ended that Saturday, the results from all over the nation began trickling in.

I was awake praying in my study at about 3 a.m. the next morning when I decided to turn on the television. The TV station had organised a panel of analysts to discuss the election results as they came in.

That dawn, I saw the whitened harvest of souls even more vividly. For the few minutes that I watched, election results came in from three major cities. In all these three major cities, the opposition party had won by very large margins. The figures showed several thousand votes in favour of the opposition party.

I thought, "Wow! The opposition seems to be winning!"

I switched off my television and concentrated on preparing for my Sunday services. By mid-morning, election results from remote towns and undeveloped districts began to roll in. This time the story was different. The ruling party was having a landslide victory. They won so many votes from rural and distant places that they completely swallowed up the victories that the opposition party had achieved in the big regional capitals. I looked at the results and noticed the names of places I had never heard of.

As I watched the elections tip in favour of the ruling party, God spoke to me. He said, "There are many more human beings out there in this nation than you can see." He added, "The real harvest is out there in the remote towns and the villages."

He showed me that masses of people are out there, far away from the big cities. I thought to myself that of the thousands of people out there in the rural areas, how many really know the Lord!

Sometimes we become happy when we have two hundred people in our city church. It is because we cannot see the extent of the harvest fields we are dealing with. **There are thousands and thousands of human beings out there beyond the main roads and beyond the cities!** Who will go there? How will they hear about Jesus Christ? How can they believe except they hear? And how can they hear the Gospel except someone goes there to preach?

> **How then shall they call on him in whom they have not believed? and how shall they believe in him of whom they have not heard? and HOW SHALL THEY HEAR WITHOUT A PREACHER?**
> **Romans 10:14**

We must become soul winners because we must all do the work of evangelists.

But watch thou in all things, endure afflictions, do the work of an evangelist, make full proof of thy ministry.
2 Timothy 4:5

Here Am I, Send Him

It is easy to get a pastor to go to New York City or Copenhagen. However, it is not so easy to get a missionary to go to one of Africa's lesser-known towns. If pastors saw the enormity of the harvest, perhaps they would realise that we need to concentrate on evangelism.

34. Soul winning is the primary work of the church.

And the gospel MUST FIRST BE PUBLISHED among all nations.
Mark 13:10

The primary role of the Church is not to build schools. That is the job of the Ministry of Education. The principal job of the Church is not to open hospitals. That is the job of the Ministry of Health. The central task of the Church is not to build orphanages. These are all good things and I believe in all of them. But none of these is the primary reason for which God raised up the Church.

How many churches have degenerated into social clubs and political groups? Someone may think that I am against hospitals and schools being set up by churches. You are wrong! Setting up schools and hospitals by churches is a good thing. I went to a Catholic school. Churches run the best schools and hospitals in Ghana. What I am saying is that it is not the *primary thing* that the Church is supposed to do. That is not our chief task. Perhaps it is a secondary or tertiary function of the Church.

Every institution must know what its principal role is! Would you be happy if you sent your child to school and the main thing he or she did was to attend long prayer services everyday without learning anything? Of course not! The school is supposed to educate the child and not to conduct all-day prayer meetings. There is nothing wrong if the school has a weekly

33

service or a daily prayer time. That is a different thing. But every institution has its primary role. **When you make a secondary role the primary function, the institution becomes completely confused and irrelevant.**

There are times when pastors come under pressure from governments and the community to change their emphasis. You will hear important government officials saying things like, "We advise the Church to become more *socially relevant* instead of praying everyday." You will hear dignitaries calling on church leaders, "We appeal to the Church to extend electricity to this town so that the contribution of the Church will be felt." "If the Church can dig some boreholes for this village, its relevance to the society will be appreciated."

Dear friend, digging boreholes and providing water for a community is not what makes the Church relevant! That is not our primary job. The Head of the Church, Jesus Christ, has given us clear instructions to GO INTO THE WORLD AND PREACH!

Preaching and teaching is the primary task of churches and ministers. Preaching and teaching the Gospel is what makes the Church relevant. I wish to emphasize this to any politician who intends to make the Church what he calls "relevant".

It is because we have lost our drive for soul winning that people have begun to see us as a sort of social institution, delivering social needs. When we preach and teach, people are saved and their lives are changed. This is our best contribution to our society!

35. You must be a soul winner because soul winning makes converts who bring about major changes in society.

Who was before a blasphemer, and a persecutor, and injurious: but I obtained mercy, because I did it ignorantly in unbelief. And the grace of our Lord was exceeding abundant with faith and love which is in Christ Jesus. This is a faithful saying, and worthy of

**all acceptation, that Christ Jesus came into the world
to save sinners; of whom I am chief.**
1 Timothy 1:13-15

The apostle Paul is the best example of someone whose conversion brought about major changes in the world.

What is the greatest canker that has destroyed most African nations? Is it not corruption? Ghana is endowed with riches, yet majority of our people are impoverished. Corruption has left its mark on the masses. The situation is so bad that entire shiploads of cocoa can disappear on the high seas. How is this possible?

A modern form of corruption involving the inflation of contract figures has surfaced in Ghana. Projects which should have cost sixteen million dollars, end up costing the nation twenty four million dollars.

Where does the eight million dollars go? Straight into private pockets! Inflated contracts are signed everyday and the nation loses millions of dollars into the pockets of vampires.

When people are born again and taught the Word of God, they refuse to be involved in corruption and other evil deeds. This is one of the areas by which the Church becomes relevant. The preaching of righteousness by the church greatly reduces corruption in the nation.

Isn't Africa the battlefield for many civil wars and conflicts? Is the Gospel not a Gospel of peace? As people hear the Word of God, do they not choose peace rather than war?

I have several former radical student leaders in my church. These people were once politically aflame, fighting authorities over any frivolous and vexatious cause they could find. Today they are peaceful born-again citizens serving and building their nation.

There is no need for the Church to leave its main duties. Dear Christian, let us never forget that we are standing in the midst of harvest fields - whitened and ripened, ready to be harvested.

I greatly respect ministers who have stayed with their original call. I recently listened to an evangelist on television. This man has conducted several crusades worldwide. I listened to him speaking about the harvest and I became excited!

I said to myself, "Thank God this man has stayed with the original call."

I Have a Vision

I have a vision: To win the lost at any cost. It is a vision that has been burning in my spirit. I want to see people saved. I do not think that the answer to humanity's needs can be found in any political solution. Neither colonisation nor independence can help us. Democracy, "house cleaning" or revolutions are not the answer to the problems of Africa or the world.

Someone asked me whether I did not want to help people by using my medical profession. I said to him, "I really do want to help people but I know that I can help them best by giving them the Gospel."

If you give a man quinine tablets and save his life, what have you really done? You have extended his life on this earth for a few more days. What about eternity? When he stands before God Almighty, the message of salvation will help much more than four tablets of chloroquine.

I am helping people much more by preaching the Gospel than by practising medicine. That is a fact; it is the reality.

Dear friend, I have a vision to plant churches anywhere I can find people. I want to win the lost at any cost. I have a vision to train as many preachers as possible. I want men and women to be as fruitful as they possibly can. I have a dream that God will use me to reap His harvest.

Thank God for doctors, teachers and politicians. Let them concentrate on their jobs, and I will concentrate on mine. I am calling on fellow ministers of the Gospel. I am calling their attention to the harvest fields that are ripened and waiting for labourers!

36. We must be soul winners so that the lost will also benefit from the great treasure of salvation.

a. Most people only acquire treasures on earth. This is foolishness.

Charge them that are rich in this world, that they be not highminded, nor trust in uncertain riches, but in the living God, who giveth us richly all things to enjoy;
1 Timothy 6:17

And he spake a parable unto them, saying, The ground of a certain rich man brought forth plentifully: And he thought within himself, saying, What shall I do, because I have no room where to bestow my fruits? And he said, This will I do: I will pull down my barns, and build greater; and there will I bestow all my fruits and my goods.
And I will say to my soul, Soul, thou hast much goods laid up for many years; take thine ease, eat, drink, and be merry. But God said unto him, Thou fool, this night thy soul shall be required of thee: then whose shall those things be, which thou hast provided?
So is he that layeth up treasure for himself, and is not rich toward God.
Luke 12:16-21

b. There are everlasting treasures found in Heaven.

But lay up for yourselves treasures in heaven, where neither moth nor rust doth corrupt, and where thieves do not break through nor steal: For where your treasure is, there will your heart be also.
Matthew 6:20-21

c. The spiritual treasures of Heaven are hidden. Heaven is hidden. The blood of Jesus is hidden. Abundant life is hidden. It is not apparent to the casual browser.

d. You must give up everything for the treasure of the kingdom.

Again, the kingdom of heaven is like unto treasure hid in a field; the which when a man hath found, he hideth, and for joy thereof goeth and selleth all that he hath, and buyeth that field.

Matthew 13:44

e. God urges everyone to pay the price for this great spiritual treasure.

Buy the truth, and sell it not; also wisdom, and instruction, and understanding.

Proverbs 23:23

Ho, every one that thirsteth, come ye to the waters, and he that hath no money; come ye, buy, and eat; yea, come, buy wine and milk without money and without price.

Isaiah 55:1

f. God offers you the treasures of His mercy, His blood, and His forgiveness.

In whom we have redemption through his blood, the forgiveness of sins, according to the riches of his grace;

Ephesians 1:7

Or despisest thou the riches of his goodness and forbearance and longsuffering; not knowing that the goodness of God leadeth thee to repentance?

Romans 2:4

g. God offers you the treasures of eternal and abundant life.

Unto me, who am less than the least of all saints, is this grace given, that I should preach among the Gentiles the unsearchable riches of Christ;

Ephesians 3:8

h. God offers you the treasures of Heaven itself.

In my Father's house are many mansions: if it were not so, I would have told you. I go to prepare a place for you. And if I go and prepare a place for you, I will come again, and receive you unto myself; that where I am, there ye may be also.

John 14:2-3

i. Pay the price today and receive the riches of Christ and salvation.

Yea doubtless, and I count all things but loss for the excellency of the knowledge of Christ Jesus my Lord: for whom I have suffered the loss of all things, and do count them but dung, that I may win Christ,

Philippians 3:8

37. You must be a soul winner so that you will become one of the stars who will shine forever.

And they that be wise shall shine as the brightness of the firmament; and they that turn many to righteousness AS THE STARS FOR EVER and ever.

Daniel 12:3

God has promised in His Word that those who win souls and those who turn many lives to Christ will enjoy a permanent status of stardom in Heaven.

The glory of the film stars and the pop stars of this world is fleeting. Some of these stars were so famous that everyone in the world knew them. Yet, a few years down the line, they were forgotten. Their names are not mentioned anymore. They are actually no longer stars.

God has promised every soul winner that he will be a star forever. Thank God that your heavenly stardom will not be a temporary one.

There are several other special rewards that are listed for those who lived and worked for Jesus.

38. You must be a soul winner so that you will be invited to dinner at the Tree of Life.

He that hath an ear, let him hear what the Spirit saith unto the churches; To him that overcometh will I give TO EAT OF THE TREE OF LIFE, which is in the midst of the paradise of God.

Revelation 2:7

There is going to be a special occasion where dinner will be served at the Tree of Life. Some of us will be invited. Do you remember when there was an important function to which you were not invited? How painful it was! Make sure that you are invited to the dinner at the Tree of Life.

These things look like insignificant prizes. One day, it will matter whether you have them or not. Everyone that overcomes in the ministry will receive this special invitation.

39. You must be a soul winner so that you will be invited to the royal family of Heaven.

...be thou faithful unto death, and I will give thee A CROWN of life.

Revelation 2:10

A crown separates royalty from the commoners! If you think there are classes on earth, please get ready for Heaven. If you think the differences between the royal family and the rest of us commoners are too great, then get ready!

Fortunately, you and I have a chance to possess a crown and become royalty in Heaven. You will have a chance to be a part of the royal family in Heaven.

Missionaries who have been faithful unto death can expect to be members of the royal family of Heaven.

40. You must be a soul winner so that you will escape damage from the second death.

He that hath an ear, let him hear what the spirit saith unto the churches; He that overcometh SHALL NOT BE HURT of the second death.
Revelation 2:11

It seems that some people will be hurt by the event of the second death. In other words, they will have some damage as they pass through this experience. The Bible teaches us that some people will be saved as through fire.

If any man's work shall be burned, he shall suffer loss: but he himself shall be saved; YET SO AS BY FIRE.
1 Corinthians 3:15

To be saved through fire means that everything gets burnt up but the individual survives. *Although you are saved you experience great loss to your property and personal possessions.* Everyone that overcomes has this great promise. You will not be hurt or experience damage through the process of the second death. I hope you see your advantages piling up as you overcome in the ministry.

41. You must be a soul winner so that you will enjoy the Hidden Manna.

...To him that overcometh will I give to eat of THE HIDDEN MANNA...
Revelation 2:17

What is hidden manna? Of what use is this hidden manna to my life? Dear friend, you do not know what pertains in Heaven. Perhaps those who have this hidden manna will have some great advantage in Heaven.

When you are a child you do not know the significance of certain things. You do not know the importance of being an American citizen. It means nothing to you as a child, but if you were a grown up you would probably appreciate having

41

U.S. citizenship. Perhaps the hidden manna will be like this - an object of great importance that you will discover only upon arriving in Heaven.

42. You must be a soul winner so that you will be given a white stone.

> **…and will give him A WHITE STONE, and in the stone a new name written, which no man knoweth saving he that receiveth it.**
>
> **Revelation 2:17**

What is this white stone and what can it do for me? Once again, we will probably discover its value when we arrive in Heaven. I can imagine why you don't think much of this white stone. After all, what is a stone on earth? But I tell you, it may be the one thing that everyone in Heaven longs for. Don't be jealous if I have a white stone and you don't!

43. Become a soul winner so that you will be appointed over nations.

> **And he that overcometh and keepeth my works unto the end, to him will I give POWER OVER THE NATIONS:**
>
> **Revelation 2:26**

I am happy to announce to you that, appointments as rulers over the different countries of the world will be given to people who do the work of the Lord. Perhaps you will be the President of Mexico. Perhaps you will be appointed over Fiji. You will sit on a throne and have an unbelievable status.

I was amazed when I read Rick Joyner's *"The Final Quest"*. All sorts of people were sitting on glorious thrones. He described how the least of these thrones were greater than any earthly throne. People were rulers over cities on earth and others were rulers over the affairs of Heaven. Others still were rulers over the affairs of the physical creation, such as the stars and galaxies.

How real these little Scriptures had become! May we not miss our thrones. Win the lost at any cost and you will be appointed over nations!

44. You must be a soul winner so that you will receive the morning star.

And he that overcometh and keepeth my works unto the end...I will give him THE MORNING STAR.
Revelation 2:26,28

This morning star is one of the rewards that we will only understand in Heaven. What the morning star will do for you, no one knows.

I assure you, however, that when you get to Heaven you will be glad if you have a morning star.

45. You must be a soul winner so that you finish all the good works that God has prepared for you to accomplish.

For we are his workmanship, created in Christ Jesus unto good works, which God hath before ordained that we should walk in them.
Ephesians 2:10

Notice the story of *Jim Sepulveda* who died on the operating table and was covered with a sheet. He came back to life after eight minutes. He was asked to return back to the earth to finish his work.

Jim Sepulveda, USA, travelled the world sharing his testimony and preaching. In March 1994, God decided it was his time and at the age of 54 he died in Canada on his way home from a preaching tour.

"It was one of those operations they do whilst you're conscious so I was awake the whole time and everything seemed to go well.

They had just got to the last manoeuvre when I suddenly felt a searing pain in the middle of my heart. This pain ran across my shoulders and down my chest and side. As I began to lose consciousness, I could feel the doctors pounding on my chest.

'Jesus, if it's my time to come home, I'm ready,' I thought. 'I love you.' I was engulfed in complete peace with no fear of death. As a dark shadow came around me, I could hear voices from far away, echoing like a tunnel: 'We're losing him…losing him…losing him…' I opened my eyes and I was standing in a field, surrounded by acres of green grass. Every blade glowed as if backlit by a tiny spotlight. To my right stretched a dazzling expanse of vibrant flowers, with colours I'd never seen before. Above me the endless sky was a deep and pure blue. The air around me was permeated with love.

I walked over a hill, a short distance away, then stopped beside the base of a large tree. A light began to appear beside the tree. The blinding aura was too bright to look at directly. I squinted down towards the ground, and then saw a pair of sandals begin to appear at the bottom edge of the light. As my eyes moved upward, I glimpsed the hem of a seamless white gown. Higher, I could make out the form of a man's body. Around his head shone an even brighter brilliance, obscuring a direct view of his face. Even though I couldn't see clearly because of the dazzling splendour, I knew immediately the identity of this man. I was standing in the presence of Jesus Christ.

'Jim, I love you.' His voice washed over me, indescribably gentle, tender, peaceful. "But it's not your time yet. *You must go back for you have many works for Me yet to do.*" I stood in awe, unable to utter a sound. Inside of me I was protesting that I was never going back, I wanted to stay right there beside Him. Almost with the hint of a chuckle, He spoke again: 'Jim, I love you, but it's not your time yet.' Then the brilliance surrounding Him reached out and engulfed me, immersing me in a sense of love and peace. I don't know how long I stood transfixed but finally I turned away and began walking over the hill. Then a blue mist of light began to come around me like a fog. It turned into a dark shadow, and everything went black.

Suddenly, I opened my eyes and realized I was lying on the operating table, covered with a sheet. I didn't know until later that I'd been clinically dead for eight minutes. Everyone had left the operating room except for the main surgeon and one of his assistants. ***They were at the back of the room, filling out a report on my death***. After a few seconds, I sat up. The sheet slid down my lap, and I saw two men at the far side of the room with their backs to me.

'Gentlemen,' I announced, 'I'm ready to proceed if you are!' They turned and looked at me, their faces white. 'Get the rest of them in here quick,' the surgeon finally said to his assistant.

They ran test after test on me. Early the next morning, the surgeon came to my room and announced he was releasing me from the hospital. 'Come back this evening at 8.30 to my office and we'll go over all the results of your new tests.'

That evening, I told my doctor what I'd experienced during those eight minutes I'd 'died' on the operating table. 'Jim,' he said after I was done, 'I'm going to show you something you won't believe.' Together we looked at the new picture of my heart. Rather than being enlarged, it was now the normal size. Where there had been 85 percent blockage in two arteries, there was now no arteriosclerosis and the main valve was functioning normally.

'We ran test after test on you, Jim!' He looked at me and winked. 'This is off the record…' I saw a tear form at the corner of his eye but he had a smile on his face. 'According to this picture, this Jesus you've been talking about has either replaced or repaired your heart'."

46. You must be a soul winner so that you will wear heavenly designer clothes.

> He that overcometh, the same shall be clothed in
> **WHITE RAIMENT…**
>
> **Revelation 3:5**

Special clothes will be provided for special people who overcome in the ministry.

At a graduation ceremony in most universities, the robes that are worn have a meaning. They signify your achievements and they signify your rank in the academic world. For instance, three bars on the sleeve of the robe often indicate a doctorate degree. As we move about in Heaven, those who have these special robes will be distinguished in their heavenly ranks by their achievements on earth. Mind you, these robes are not given to everyone but to "him that overcometh". Win the lost at any cost!

47. You must be a soul winner so that you will receive divine recommendation.

He that overcometh…I WILL CONFESS HIS NAME before my Father, and before his angels.
Revelation 3:5

Upon arriving in Heaven, you may or may not receive a special recommendation by Jesus to the Father. In the army for instance, after a war is over, you may be recommended by your Commanding Officer. If you are recommended to the government for your bravery, you receive awards like a Purple Heart or a Congressional Medal of Honour. Dear friend, recommendations are going to be made after the last battle is over. Will your Commanding Officer have anything on which to recommend you? I pray so!

In receiving this award, you will be taken to the Father in the presence of angels and be highly commended to the Father for your good works. This will be done in the presence of angels and the hosts of Heaven. You can understand why you would be respected by all and sundry, if Jesus singles you out and says to the Father, "This was a special son who did more than his share, please accord him a special status in Heaven." I tell you man, you are covered! It is not everyone who will receive such a recommendation.

Dear Christian, please aim for these glorious rewards. Win the lost at any cost and you will be recommended by Jesus to the Father.

48. You must be a soul winner so that you will receive a divine autograph.

Him that overcometh will I make a pillar in the temple of my God, and he shall go no more out: and I will write upon him the name of my God, and the name of the city of my God, which is new Jerusalem...and I WILL WRITE UPON HIM MY NEW NAME.

Revelation 3:12

Dear friend, people "buy" names all the time. The MacDonald's name or franchise is acquired for a lot of money. Polo shirts, t-shirts, belts and shoes carry names that make people buy them.

It is not strange that one of the rewards given to some privileged people will be to have the label of God's name on them.

Perhaps your robe will be labelled *El' Shaddai*. Perhaps your designer clothes will be labelled *Elohim*. Maybe your belt will be labelled *Jehovah Nissi*. When people recognize this powerful signature on you, you will be distinguished from others in Heaven.

49. You must be a soul winner because Jesus is standing at the door of the heart of a sinner and is knocking.

Behold, I stand at the door, and knock: if any man hear my voice, and open the door, I will come in to him, and will sup with him, and he with me.

Revelation 3:20

50. You must be a soul winner so that you will receive heavenly positions.

To him that overcometh will I grant to sit with me in my throne, even as I also overcame, and am SET DOWN WITH MY FATHER IN HIS THRONE.

Revelation 3:21

Promotion into unbelievable heights awaits you as you do God's will. You will be elevated to the highest of positions according to this Scripture. Perhaps you don't know the value of being on a throne. After all, you have never been on anything like a throne on earth. Perhaps you think you can manage without such a privilege. Don't let the devil deceive you. You must not miss this great reward. You must win the lost at any cost!

51. You must be a soul winner so that God will be gracious and bless you.

When you win souls, God will bless you because He wants His salvation to be known to all nations. God will make His face shine on you because you are a soul winner.

> **God be gracious to us and bless us, And cause His face to shine upon us -- Selah. That Your way may be known on the earth, Your salvation among all nations.**
>
> **Psalm 67:1-2, NASB**

52. You must be a soul winner and overcome the sin of ethnocentricism.

When you suffer from the sin of ethnocentricism you carry a belief that your particular race, tribe or nationality is superior to all others. The apostles in Judea suffered from this and did not reach out to people who were not Jews.

> **The apostles and the brothers throughout Judea heard that the Gentiles also had received the word of God.**
> **So when Peter went up to Jerusalem, the circumcised believers criticised him and said, "You went into the house of uncircumcised men and ate with them." Peter began and explained everything to them precisely as it had happened:**
>
> **Acts 11:1-4, NIV**

53. You must become a soul winner to avoid the mistake of fishing in a bathtub.

a. Peter fished for souls in the streets of Jerusalem.

**And by the hands of the apostles were many signs and
wonders wrought among the people; (and they were
all with one accord in Solomon's porch. And of the
rest durst no man join himself to them: but the people
magnified them.
And believers were the more added to the Lord,
multitudes both of men and women.)
Insomuch that they brought forth the sick into the
streets, and laid them on beds and couches, that
at the least the shadow of Peter passing by might
overshadow some of them.
There came also a multitude out of the cities round
about unto Jerusalem, bringing sick folks, and them
which were vexed with unclean spirits: and they were
healed every one.**

Acts 5:12-16

b. Philip fished for souls in the despised town of Samaria.
Every experienced soul winner will avoid hard and
unyielding fields.

**Then Philip went down to the city of Samaria, and
preached Christ unto them.
And the people with one accord gave heed unto those
things which Philip spake, hearing and seeing the
miracles which he did. For unclean spirits, crying
with loud voice, came out of many that were possessed
with them: and many taken with palsies, and that
were lame, were healed. And there was great joy in
that city.**

Acts 8:5-8

**Say not ye, There are yet four months, and then
cometh harvest? behold, I say unto you, Lift up your
eyes, and look on the fields; FOR THEY ARE WHITE
ALREADY TO HARVEST.**

John 4:35

Jesus, the master soul winner understood the concept of ripened and unripened harvest fields. He described the ripened harvest fields as being "white unto harvest".

When you get involved with the task of soul winning, you will quickly begin to direct your efforts away from unripened fields. People who are not soul winners are comfortable in unripened fields but a true harvester is always looking for fields that are ready.

c. Paul fished for souls on Mars Hill.

Then Paul stood in the midst of Mars' hill, and said, Ye men of Athens, I perceive that in all things ye are too superstitious.

Acts 17:22

d. Paul fished for souls on the Melita island.

And when they were escaped, then they knew that the island was called Melita.
And the barbarous people shewed us no little kindness: for they kindled a fire, and received us every one, because of the present rain, and because of the cold.

Acts 28:1-2

It is a mistake to try to harvest fields that are not ready. Every soul winner must know that God's harvest fields are ripe at different times. Doors to certain regions are divinely opened for a season. After a while, these doors swing shut.

54. To avoid the mistake of sowing my seed on a hard stony floor.

Stay with the ripened harvest. Go where the doors are open. That is why I love preaching to young people. Every year I hold special programmes in each of the universities in Ghana. I enjoy preaching in secondary schools. I see such a positive response from the young people. The young people are my ripened harvest.

I remember speaking with an eighty-year-old man at a wedding reception. During the wedding service, I had preached a sermon on salvation. This man was in the congregation and had heard all that I had said.

He called me aside at the wedding reception and said to me, "I want you to know something."

"What is it, sir?" I asked.

He answered, "I want you to know that I will never change!"

"Oh!" I responded.

"I Will Never Be Born Again!"

He continued, "I am eighty years old and I will never change! I want you to know that I will never be born again! I am a traditionalist, I belong to the Anglican Church and I will never be born again!"

I was taken aback! I had never heard anybody speak like that. This man was saying that he was hardened and resistant to the Gospel. There are many people like that. Preaching to them yields very little result.

Stay with the ripened and whitened harvests. God will bless your evangelistic efforts. The poor are often more open to receive the Gospel than the rich. Therefore, preach more to the poor than to the rich.

When you spend time on unripened harvests, you will become discouraged with evangelism. You will find it fruitless and a waste of time. Stay with the ripened harvests. God has given them to you! Win the lost at any cost!

55. Soul winning was the FIRST COMMAND of Jesus Christ to all of us, His disciples.

The first thing that Jesus told His disciples when He met them was:

...Follow me, and I will make you fishers of men.

Matthew 4:19

The whole idea of taking Peter and John away from their learned trade of fishing was to make them harvesters of souls.

56. Soul winning was the LAST COMMAND of Jesus Christ to all of us, His disciples.

On a lonely hill with eleven disciples, Jesus issued His last emotional command.

And he said unto them, GO YE INTO ALL THE WORLD, and preach the gospel to every creature.

Mark 16:15

What Were Jesus' Last Words?

The last words of a man are probably the most important words that he will ever speak. Some years ago, I read about an aircraft that developed a serious problem. As it flew over some mountains, the pilot informed everyone on board that they were going to crash; indeed they crashed and everyone on board was killed. It seemed as if they had about ten or fifteen minutes before they eventually crashed. Many of the passengers wrote notes and messages to their loved ones while they could. I will never forget that scene on television. I couldn't help but wonder what those last messages and notes contained. Anyone who knows he's going away forever would probably give a very important message as his last word.

So what were Jesus' last words? Did Jesus say, "Go and make people rich?" Did he say, "Go and build hospitals and schools?" Did he say, "Go and take the reins of political power?" He did not! He said the Church should go out and preach the Gospel in as many countries as possible. He told us to travel far and wide with the good news of the kingdom.

57. You must be a soul winner because *Oswald J. Smith* said, "No one has the right to hear the Gospel twice while there remains someone who has not heard it once."

58. You must be a soul winner because *Oswald J. Smith* said, "Any church that is not seriously involved in fulfilling the Great Commission has forfeited its biblical right to exist."

In other words, only as the church fulfils her missionary obligation does she justify her existence.

59. You must be soul winner because *Oswald J. Smith* said, "We talk of the second coming when half the world has never heard of the first coming."

60. You must be a soul winner because *Keith Green* said, "This generation of Christians is responsible for this generation of souls on the earth."

61. You must be a soul winner because *C.T. Studd* said, "If Jesus Christ be God and died for me then no sacrifice can be too great for me to make for Him."

62. You must be a soul winner because *Keith Wright* said, "Lost people matter to God and so they must matter to us."

63. You must be a soul winner because *J.G. Morrison*, pleading with Nazarenes in the 1930s Great Depression to support their missionaries said, "Can't you do just a little bit more?"

64. You must be a soul winner because *David Livingstone,* missionary to Africa, said, "Sympathy is no substitute for action."

65. You must be a soul winner because *David Livingstone* said, "If a commission by an earthly king is an honour, how can a commission by a heavenly king be considered a sacrifice?"

66. You must be a soul winner because there are thousands of places where no soul winner has ever been.

Robert Moffat (who inspired David Livingstone) said, "In the vast plain to the north I have sometimes seen, in the morning sun, the smoke of a thousand villages where no missionary has ever been."

67. You must be a soul winner because if the Holy Spirit is in us we must have big visions and dreams of winning souls for the Lord.

And it shall come to pass in the last days, saith God, I will pour out of my Spirit upon all flesh: and your sons and your daughters shall prophesy, and your young men shall see visions, and your old men shall dream dreams:

Acts 2:17

Francis Xavier, missionary to India said, "Tell the students to give up their small ambitions and come eastward to preach the Gospel of Christ"

68. You must be a soul winner because we must take up our crosses and follow the example of Christ, who died fulfilling the will of God.

Then said Jesus unto his disciples, If any man will come after me, let him deny himself, and take up his cross, and follow me.

Matthew 16:24

When *James Calvert* went out as a missionary to the cannibals of the Fiji Islands, the ship captain tried to turn him back saying, "You will lose your life and the lives of those with you if you go among such savages." To that, Calvert replied, "We died before we came here."

69. You must be a soul winner because *John Keith Falconer* said, "I have but one candle of life to burn and I would rather burn it out in a land filled with darkness than in a land flooded with light."

70. You must be a soul winner because *William Carey* (the father of modern missions) said, "Expect great things from God, attempt great things for God."

71. You must be a soul winner because *Henry Martyn,* missionary to India and Persia said, "The spirit of Christ is the spirit of missions. The nearer we get to Him, the more intensely missionary we become."

72. You must be a soul winner because *Hudson Taylor,* missionary to China said, "The Great Commission is not an option to be considered. It is a command to be obeyed."

73. You must be a soul winner because *Dave Davidson* said, "If you found a cure for cancer, wouldn't it be inconceivable to hide it from the rest of mankind. How much more inconceivable to keep silent the cure from the eternal wages of death."

In the day of good news, the lepers did not keep silent and hide it from the rest of the starving. We must not keep silent and hide it from the rest of the world.

> Therefore they arose and fled to the twilight, and left their tents and their horses and their donkeys, even the camp just as it was, and fled for their life.
> When these lepers came to the outskirts of the camp, they entered one tent and ate and drank, and carried from there silver and gold and clothes, and went and hid them; and they returned and entered another tent and carried from there also, and went and hid them.
> Then they said to one another, "WE ARE NOT DOING RIGHT. THIS IS A DAY OF GOOD NEWS, BUT WE ARE KEEPING SILENT; if we wait until morning light, punishment will overtake us. Now therefore come, let us go and tell the king's household."
>
> **2 Kings 7:7-9, NASB**

74. You must be a soul winner because *Dave Davidson* said, "In our lifetime wouldn't it be sad if we spent more time washing dishes or swatting flies or mowing the yard or watching television than praying for world missions?"

75. You must be a soul winner because God does not want anyone to perish in Hell.

The Lord is not slack concerning his promise, as some men count slackness; but is longsuffering to us-ward, NOT WILLING THAT ANY SHOULD PERISH, but that all should come to repentance.

2 Peter 3:9

For God so loved the world, that he gave his only begotten Son, that whosoever believeth in him SHOULD NOT PERISH, but have everlasting life.

John 3:16

The story of **Rev. Ron Reagan** and his experience of seeing his brothers burning in Hell is a frightening reminder about how unsaved people are perishing in Hell:

"One day I decided to take my little son, Ronnie Paul, to a town called Pigeon Ford, and a little market there. As I started to go through the entrance door to the market, another man was coming out. He wouldn't back off and neither would I. The hatred and violence just rose up in me and I busted his head right in the doorway. He fell into a stacked up case of bottles and they burst and went all over the store.

People were screaming and running, but he picked up a broken bottle and came swinging for my face. As I lifted my left arm to try and stop the blow, he severed all the ligaments, tendons and the artery in my arm. In a fit of rage, I hit him again and kicked at him but this time with that bottle, he severed the achilles tendon and the arteries in my leg. In minutes the blood was pumping out of my body like out of a water hole.

Every time my heart beat the blood would squirt out and I quickly became faint. The man who ran the market told me that unless I got to the hospital quickly I would be dead.

So he got me into the passenger side of my car while he drove, whilst my young son, watching it all, was screaming - completely hysterical. By the time we reached the hospital the floor well of the passenger side was awash with my blood - my feet were wallowing in it. I could hear voices but couldn't open my eyes anymore, because all my strength had gone. When they rolled me into the emergency room I could hear the doctors and nurses saying, 'He's going to need extensive surgery. Transfer him to the hospital in Knoxville.' They loaded me into the ambulance and got me ready for transfer to Knoxville.

Someone had got hold of Elaine and she rushed to the hospital and got into the ambulance with me, as we set off. A young man, about 21 or 22 , the paramedic, looked in my face and said, 'Sir, do you know Jesus Christ?' I cursed him and God, with all the strength left in my body. 'There is no God. Who is this Jesus you are talking about? Look at me. Do you think there is a God?' The young man just looked at me and said, 'He loves you, Jesus will help you. Call on Him.' Something inside of me caused me to foam and spit and cry out, 'God, if You really exist, help me. I can't help myself. Help me please.' The young man continued saying, 'Jesus died for you, He gave His life for you.' And all the time I listened, I could hear my wife sobbing.

Smoke filled the ambulance. I couldn't breath, I couldn't see. I thought the ambulance was on fire! What's wrong?' **I called out, 'I can't see.'** Then through the smoke I started hearing different voices, 'Razor. Razor Reagan. Ronnie! **Turn around, don't come here. Go back, stop now. Don't come here!'** As I kept hearing these voices, the smoke opened up and I could see what looked like the old quarry pit that we used to swim in when I was a child. In fact it looked exactly like it did on the night we poured gasoline into it and set the water on fire. It was burning and blazing and I was getting nearer to that pit. **I could see people in there, and they were burning. Their arms, their faces, their bodies were blazing and the fire wasn't going out.** And they were screaming my name!

Closer and closer I went until I could see the individuals, but I couldn't understand what I was seeing. **There were two standing close together and I saw they were Billy and Freddy, my two brothers, and they were burning and screaming. 'What are you doing here?' I yelled, 'You died on the highway in a 1957 Chevrolet, drunk, when you hit the block wall doing 100mph.** What are you doing here?' They said, **'Don't come here, there's no way out, It's horrible. Don't come here!!'**

I looked to the side. **'Oh, no. Charles! Charles, what are you doing here?** Last time I saw you, you were in Pigeon River. We couldn't get the car off you because we were all drunk. When you went into the river we couldn't get you out! We saw your face looking up through the water but we couldn't get you out!'

'Go back', he said, 'Don't come here.'

I looked and could see flower children standing against the wall just like I'd seen them in the sixties, dazed. Flower children so blown away. The age of Aquarius! And I saw many that had overdosed and died. Then I saw my friend, Richard. **'Oh Richard, I can't help you.** When we robbed the liquor store in Atlanta, you didn't know what you were doing. You had an old pistol that didn't have any bullets in it and you didn't even ask for the money. But the man didn't know your gun wasn't loaded and he reached under the counter and pulled out a 357, fired point blank and blew your heart out of your chest. You fell against a parking meter and slipped down in the broken glass with the wine and the blood spilling over you. The last thing you said was, **'Oh God.' Richard cried out, 'Don't come here. You can't help.'**

I cannot convey the horror, the terror of what I saw and heard. All I knew was I didn't understand it. Suddenly everything went black and I woke up.

Forty-eight hours later I came round in the hospital. My wife was sitting beside me. I had hundreds of stitches inside and outside my body. My wife explained that the doctors had decided not to amputate my arm in view of my job as a truck driver. They would keep a close watch on it though. But I wasn't interested in my arm because I remembered what I'd seen. I could not forget!

People now ask me why I cry, run, and dance when I preach. And I think, 'Oh, Jesus, if it happened to them how it happened to me, they'd know why I'm like I am. Oh God, I don't want to hate anybody no more, I don't want to shoot anybody no more. Oh God, I love everybody'."

76. You must be a soul winner because the founder of World Vision, *Bob Pierce* said, "Let my heart be broken with the things that break God's heart."

In the story of the prodigal son, the elder brother did not have the same passion as his father. His father was looking out for the lost but the elder brother was not even happy to see his lost brother come home. Many Christians have hearts which are not moved with the things that move God's heart.

77. You must be a soul winner because God loved the whole world so much that He gave His only Son to die for us.

For God so loved the world, that he gave his only begotten Son, that whosoever believeth in him should not perish, but have everlasting life.

John 3:16

78. You must be a soul winner because Carl F. H. Henry said, "The Gospel is only good news if it gets there in time."

79. You must be a soul winner because the fields are ripe now unto the harvest.

Say not ye, There are yet four months, and then cometh harvest? behold, I say unto you, Lift up your eyes, and look on the fields; for they are white already to harvest.

John 4:35

Kurt von Schleicher said, "Our God of grace often gives us a second chance, but there is no second chance to harvest a ripe crop."

80. **You must be a soul winner because *Jim Elliot*, a missionary martyr who lost his life in the late 1950s trying to reach the Auca Indians of Ecuador said, "He is no fool who gives up what he cannot keep to gain that which he cannot lose."**

81. **You must be a soul winner because you do not want to be a Christian witch or wizard.**

    For rebellion is as the sin of witchcraft, and stubbornness is as iniquity and idolatry. Because thou hast rejected the word of the LORD, he hath also rejected thee from being king.
    1 Samuel 15:23

Robert Speer, a leader in student volunteer movement said, "There is nothing in the world or the church - except the church's disobedience, to render the evangelization of the world in this generation an impossibility."

82. **You must be a soul winner because *J.L. Ewen* said, "As long as there are millions destitute of the Word of God and knowledge of Jesus Christ, it will be impossible for me to devote time and energy to those who have both."**

83. **You must be a soul winner because *Robert Savage* of the Latin American mission said, "The command has been to go, but we have stayed - in body, gifts, prayer and influence. He has asked us to be witnesses unto the uttermost parts of the earth... but 99% of Christians have kept puttering around in the homeland."**

84. **You must be a soul winner because every other job has no eternal significance.**

    Therefore, my beloved brethren, be ye stedfast, unmoveable, always abounding in the work of the

Lord, forasmuch as ye know that your labour IS NOT
IN VAIN in the Lord.

1 Corinthians 15:58

85. You must be a soul winner because *Nate Saint*, a
missionary martyr, said, "People who do not know
the Lord ask why in the world we waste our lives as
missionaries. They forget that they too are expending
their lives...and when the bubble has burst, they will
have nothing of eternal significance to show for the
years they have wasted."

86. You must be a soul winner because Jesus did not come
to condemn the world and we are not yet condemned
until we die without Christ.

The story of *Dr. Maurice Rawlings* illustrates how after death,
you are condemned to Hell because you did not believe in Christ.

Dr Maurice Rawlings is a specialist in heart disease. He is
the clinical assistant professor of medicine for the University
of Tennessee at Chattanooga, a member of the International
Committee on Cardiovascular Diseases, a past governor for
the American College of Cardiology for the state of Tennessee,
founder of the area's regional Emergency Medical Services
Council, faculty instructor for the Advanced Cardiac Life
Support programmes, and Fellow of the American College of
Physicians, the College of Cardiology, and the College of Chest
Physicians. He has also been the personal doctor to Pentagon
staff, including Dwight Eisenhower.

He is the author of several books on near-death experiences
and a contributor to many medical journals. He tells this story:

"Several years ago now, I had to resuscitate a patient who
died whilst trying to reproduce by exercise the chest pains he
had been suffering - that experience changed both our lives
forever.

The man, a 47-year-old postman, was exercising on the
hospital treadmill. We were hoping the exercise would

reproduce the chest pains he said he had been getting while exercising at home. But instead of just getting the pain, the electro cardiogram (the machine that shows your heartbeat) went haywire and he dropped dead, his body thrown off the still moving treadmill. I was doing the external heart compressions while the nurses sorted out a drip and breathing bag, and the patient kept saying, 'Doctor, don't stop!' Whenever I stopped to reach for something, he would scream, 'I'm in Hell again!' Most patients would say, 'Take your big hands off, you're breaking my ribs,' so I knew something was wrong. We had to put a pacemaker down his collarbone vein right there on the floor. He was writhing and blood was spurting everywhere. I was pushing and I told him to shut up and not to bother me with his 'hell business'. I was trying to save his life and he was trying to tell me about some nefarious nightmare he was having whilst in the death throes.

He then asked me something which was the ultimate insult to me as an atheist, which was, 'Doctor, pray for me.' I told him he was out of his mind, I wasn't a minister. Again he asked me to pray for him and the nurses were looking at me with anticipation and a 'you must do it, it's a dying man's wish' look. So I did. I made up a make-believe prayer, a nonsense. I just wanted to get him off my back so I told him to say it after me. I blurted out embarrassed, 'I believe Jesus Christ is the Son of God. Go on say it. Please keep me out of hell. Say it! And if I live, I'm on the hook, I'm yours forever.' I remember that part well because he's been 'on the hook' ever since. Each time we interrupted the heart massage to adjust the pacemaker he'd scream he was back in hell, then he would convulse, turn blue, stop breathing, and his heart would stop beating.

But soon after I said the prayer there was no more writhing, no more fighting. He was calm. The next day, still highly sceptical, I asked him to tell me about being in Hell. I told him he had frightened the nurses to death and scared the hell out of me. He said, 'What Hell? After that prayer you said, I remember seeing my mother when she was living, although she had died when I was three years old.' Impossible! He picked her out of a photograph album his aunt brought in next day, but he had never actually seen her. He identified her from her clothing. He had seen her in Heaven. What apparently happened was that he had sublimated the Hell experiences to painless parts of his memory, but after the conversion he had Heaven experiences.

That 'nonsensical' prayer I prayed to humour him not only got the man converted but it got me too. We both became born-again Christians."

87. You must be a soul winner because there are many fools in this world who think that there is no God and someone must tell them about Jesus.

The fool hath said in his heart, There is no God. They are corrupt, they have done abominable works, there is none that doeth good.

Psalm 14:1

The story of the Art Professor **Howard Storm** illustrates how many people think there is no God but will be surprised when they die:

"The date was June 1985, and I was in France. I was leading a group of students on an art tour, my wife was with me and it had come to the last day of our trip. In mid-sentence, I fell to the ground, screaming with intense pain in my stomach. An ambulance came and I was rushed to hospital, to be told by the doctor that I had a hole in my duodenum, and I needed an operation. It was a Saturday, I was taken to hospital and given a bed.

With the pain getting increasingly worse, a nurse came into the room and told me and my wife that they were going to do the operation. At that point I was ready to die. I had hung on, by my fingernails as it were, trying to stay alive, but not anymore.

The problem for me was that I was an atheist. As a teenager, brought up in a liberal Protestant church, I had lost faith and at college became a scientific atheist. Now, facing death, I felt nothing but hopelessness, depression and despair. I felt I was ready to die and I knew that meant I would cease to exist. I told my wife, who was not an atheist, and did have some faith, and she was in tears.

I closed my eyes and became unconscious. I don't know how much time elapsed but I found myself standing next to my body. I opened my eyes and there was a body in my bed. I didn't understand how it was possible to be outside of one's body and yet looking at the body in my bed. Not only that, but I was extremely agitated and upset because I was yelling at my wife to get her attention but she neither saw nor heard me and didn't move at all. I turned to my room-mate but got the same reaction - he too was oblivious to me and I became more and more angry and agitated. It was at that point that I heard voices calling me by name, from outside the room. Initially I was afraid but the voices seemed friendly, and when I went to the doorway of my room I could see figures moving around in a haze; I asked them to come closer, but they wouldn't come close enough for me to see them clearly. I was able to make out only their silhouettes and general feature. These beings kept asking me to come with them and although I asked a lot of specific questions, they evaded them all giving only vague answers, but insisted that I went with them. So I reluctantly agreed.

I continued to ask questions such as where were we going and they told me that I would see when we got there. I then asked who they were and they said they had come to take me. So I followed them and we went on a journey that I know lasted many, many miles. There was no landscape or architecture, just an ever thickening, ever darkening, haze. Even though they refused to tell me where we were going, they implied they would take care of me and had something for me.

Gradually, they became increasingly cruel as it began to get ever darker. The creatures also started making fun of me and some would say to others, 'Hey, be careful, don't scare him off, or, 'Hush it's too soon for that.' What was even worse, they started making vulgar jokes about me. It seemed at first there were about a dozen of these creatures but later on I thought maybe forty or fifty. Still later, it appeared as if there were hundreds or more.

At this point, I said I wasn't going any further. This was a kind of bluff on my part because I didn't know which way was back, or where I was. I couldn't figure out how I could still be in the hospital but have walked as far as I had. The creatures responded by pushing and shoving me and at first I fought back well and was able to hit them in the face and kick them. However, I couldn't inflict any hurt on them and they simply laughed. Then they began with their finger nails and teeth to pick little pieces off me. I experienced real physical pain and this went on for a long time, with me fighting and trying to fend them off. The difficulty was that I was in the centre of a huge crowd, hands and teeth all around me, and the more I screamed and struggled, the better they liked it. The noise was terrible, as was the cruel laughter and constant torment. Then they went further, insulting me and violating me in other ways too horrible to talk about and with conversation which was more gross than could ever be imagined. Eventually I no longer had the strength or ability to fight anymore and I fell to the ground. They appeared to lose interest in me. People seemed to be coming by and giving me a kick but the intense fury had gone.

As I lay there I had the strangest experience. A voice that seemed to come from my chest spoke to my mind. This was an internal conversation and the voice said, 'Pray to God.'

I proceeded to argue with my voice, saying I didn't believe in God so how could I pray to Him. But my voice said, 'Pray to God,' and I thought, 'But I don't know how to pray, I don't know what praying means!' For a third time my voice said, 'Pray to God', so I thought I'd better try. I started to think things like 'The Lord is my Shepherd, God bless America', just little things that I could remember which sounded holy. Soon the thoughts became mutterings and as they did the creatures around me started screaming and yelling at me that there was no God. They told me I was the worst of the worst.

Nobody could hear me they said, so what did I think I was doing?

Because these evil creatures were so strong in their protest I started to say more, and shouted things at them like, 'God loves me. Get away from me. In the name of God, leave me alone!' They continued to scream at me except now they were retreating back into the darkness. I finally came to the point where I found myself screaming all the things I could think of that sounded religious but there was nobody around. I was completely alone in the darkness; they had retreated as if my words were pouring scalding water on them.

Although I was shouting little pieces of Psalm 23, 'Yea though I walk through the valley of death, I will fear no evil', and the Lord's Prayer, I didn't believe them. I meant them in the sense that I could see they were having the effect of driving these creatures off, but I wasn't convinced in my heart about the truth of them.

I was there alone. For how long, I don't know, but I sank into great hopelessness, deeper than I could imagine possible. Here I was, in the dark and somewhere out in the darkness were the evil creatures. I couldn't move, I couldn't crawl, I was too torn up and didn't know what to do. In fact I got to the point where I really did not want to exist anymore.

It was at the moment of deepest despair that a tune from my childhood, when I had gone to Sunday school, started going through my head. 'Jesus loves me…Jesus loves me, this I know', and I wanted that to be true more than I have ever wanted anything in my life. With every ounce of my being, my mind, strength and heart, I screamed into the darkness, 'Please Jesus, save me!' I meant it. I didn't question or doubt it, I just meant it with every fibre of my being and upon doing that a small faint star appeared in the darkness. It grew rapidly bright and brighter, and soon it was a large, indescribably brilliant light, which picked me into itself. As it lifted me up I looked down at myself and saw all the rips, tears and wounds that I had received, just slowly disappear. As I continued to be lifted up, I became whole and well. The only way I can describe it is as something of inexplicable beauty which I knew was good.

One minute I was an atheist, the next minute every part of me wanted Jesus. I lost all of my pride, my egotism, my self-dependence, my reliance on my much exalted intellect. All of that had ceased to serve me anymore - it had failed me. All the things I had lived my life for and made my god and had worshipped had let me down. What I came to cry out for was a hope that was planted in a small child many years before.

This experience changed my life completely. Not only did I eventually become a full-time minister but it changed the way I felt. Before there used to be melancholy and cynicism, but now there is genuine joy, all the time. That's not to say I don't have my ups and downs, but behind every day there is joyfulness and I try, as best as I can, to spread that joy and peace."

88. You must be a soul winner because *Robert C. Shannon* said, "Never pity missionaries, envy them. They are where the real action is - where life and death, sin and grace, Heaven and Hell converge."

89. You must be a soul winner because of the blood of Jesus that was shed for all nations, tribes and peoples.

And they sung a new song, saying, Thou art worthy to take the book, and to open the seals thereof: for thou wast slain, and hast redeemed us to God by thy blood out of every kindred, and tongue, and people, and nation; And hast made us unto our God kings and priests: and we shall reign on the earth.

Revelation 5:9-10

90. You must be a soul winner because Count Nicolaus *Ludwig von Zinzendorf* said, "I have but one passion: it is He, it is He alone. The world is the field and the field is the world; and henceforth that country shall be my home where I can be most used in winning souls for Christ."

91. **You must be a soul winner because *J. Howard Edington* said, "People who don't believe in missions have not read the New Testament. The early church took Him at His word and went east, west, north and south."**

92. **You must be a soul winner because *A.B. Simpson* said, "The Christian is not obedient unless he is doing all in his power to send the Gospel to the heathen world."**

93. **You must be a soul winner because John 3:16 says that Jesus died for the whole world, not a part of the world.**

Pat Morley said, "If the Great Commission is true, our plans are not too big. They are too small."

94. **You must be a soul winner because *Ted Engstrom* of World Vision said, "A congregation that is not deeply and earnestly involved in the worldwide proclamation of the Gospel does not understand the nature of salvation."**

95. **You must be a soul winner because about 6,000 people died in the last hour and entered into eternity whilst you were reading this book.**

96. **You must be a soul winner because about 143,000 people will enter eternity within the next twenty-four hours.**

97. **You must be a soul winner because in a week's time one million people will have gone out of this world into Heaven or Hell and will never have the chance to change their situation.**

The story of *Ian McCormack* of New Zealand shows how easily and quickly people pass into eternity:

"My whole life was centred around sport and travel. At 24 years of age, having taken a veterinary science degree at university in New Zealand, I had just completed two years travelling around the world. Now I was living in an earthly paradise for anyone who loved surfing and scuba diving - Mauritius.

I used to go surfing and fishing with the local Creole divers and got hooked on night diving. Being used to colder climates than the locals, I only wore a thin 1mm short-sleeved wet suit whereas the locals would wear the full 3-4mm suits and be totally encased from head to foot. Four days before I was due to leave the island and go back to New Zealand for my brother's wedding, I went out night diving with the local boys. I was a bit uneasy about going because I could see an electric storm on the horizon but I let myself be persuaded.

As I dived that night, the beam of my torch light picked out a jellyfish right in front of me. I was fascinated because this one was not the usual shape but 'box-shaped.' Little did I realize as I squeezed it through my leather-gloved hand, that this box jelly-fish, or sea wasp, was the second deadliest creature known to man. Its toxin has killed over seventy Australians alone and up in the northern parts of Australia, it had killed more people than had sharks. In Darwin, the sting from this fish stopped the heart of a 38-year-old man in 10 minutes.

Suddenly, I experienced what I felt like a huge electric shock in my forearm, like thousands of volts of electricity. Not being able to see what had happened, I did the worst thing possible, I rubbed my arm, and rubbed in the poison from the tentacles of this fish. Before I could get out onto the reef, I was stung by three other box jellyfish. My forearm was swollen like a balloon and where the tentacles had stung there were burn-like blisters across my arm. I felt on fire as the poison began moving round my body. It hit my lymph gland, as if it had been punched, and my breathing quickly became constricted.

I knew I needed hospitalization and quickly! After I was stung a fifth time, one of the divers rowed me back to shore and dumped me on the road, which was in a desolate part of the island. Lying on my back and feeling the poison taking its effect, I heard a quiet voice saying, 'Son, if you close your eyes you will never wake again.' I had no idea who said it but being a qualified lifeguard and instructor in scuba, I knew unless I got anti-toxin quickly, I would die.

My attempts to get to hospital were fraught to say the least, I had no money and an Indian taxi driver, whom I had begged on my knees for a lift, picked me up but only took me to a hotel and dumped me in the car park thinking he was unlikely to get paid. The Chinese proprietor of the hotel also refused to take me in his car, thinking the marks on my arm were from overdosing on heroin. However, a security guard, who happened to be one of my drinking companions rang for an ambulance.

During the journey, my life flashed before me and I thought, 'I'm going to die. This is what happens before you die, your life comes before you.' Despite being an atheist, I wondered whether there was any life after death. Then my mother's face came before me and said, 'Ian, no matter how far from God you are, if you will only but cry out to God from your heart, God will hear you and God will forgive you.'

I promised God however, that if I came through this experience alive, I would find out what His will for me was and follow Him all the days of my life. As I prayed that prayer I knew I had made peace with God and almost immediately the ambulance doors opened. I was lifted onto a wheelchair and raced into the hospital.

Doctors and nurses rushed in. They attempted to take my blood pressure twice, but they could find no pulse. The doctors gave me injections of anti-toxin and dextrose in an attempt to save my life.

I was conscious of the fact that if I drifted out of my body that would be it - death. I knew this was no weird trip or hallucination, this was real, but I had no intention of leaving my body and dying. I intended to stay awake all night if necessary, and fight the poison in my system.

Feeling myself being lifted onto a recovery bed, I was aware that I could not feel my arms at all and I could no longer keep my eyes open. I couldn't tilt my head, my eyes were filling up with perspiration so that I could hardly see and I remember closing my eyes and breathing a sigh of relief. At that point, from what I can ascertain from the hospital, I was clinically dead for 15 minutes.

The most scary thing for me was that the moment my eyes closed I was suddenly wide awake again, standing by what I thought was my bed, in pitch black darkness, wondering why the doctors had turned out the lights. I decided to switch the lights on and put my hand out to find the wall but I couldn't find a wall. 'OK,' I thought, 'maybe they've moved me to the general ward.' If I could get back to my bed, I could turn the lamp on but I couldn't find my bed. I thought I'd better just stand still for a moment, but it was so dark I couldn't even see my hand in front of my face and if I lifted my right hand up to my face it seemed either to miss it or go straight through. 'You can't miss your head,' I thought to myself, so I put both hands up to my face and they seemed to pass straight through. That was the most weird feeling but what followed was even worse because I realized I could not touch any part of my physical form. Yet I had the sensation of being a complete human being with all my faculties, only I didn't have a fleshly form.

I realize now that I was in fact outside my body because when someone dies, their spirit leaves their body.

My next thought was, 'Where on earth am I?' because I could feel the most intense evil pervading the darkness all around me. It was as if the darkness took on a spiritual dimension. There was a totally evil presence there, which started to move towards me. Although I still couldn't see, I sensed something looking at me out of the darkness. Then to my right came a voice which yelled, 'Shut up!' As I backed off from that voice another one from the left shouted, 'You deserve to be here!' My arms came up to protect myself and I asked, 'Where am I?' and a third voice replied, 'You're in Hell. Now shut up.' Some people think Hell is just a big party but I tell you it's going to be pretty hard to grab your beer down there and pretty hard to find your face.

I stood there in that blackness long enough to put the fear of God into me for eternity. You might ask why God took me down there, but He told me later that if I hadn't prayed that deathbed prayer in the ambulance, I would have stayed in

Hell. Thank God for His grace, which hears a sinner's prayer in the last seconds of his life."

98. **You must be a soul winner because 35,000 people died today having lived their entire lives on this planet and never once heard the name of Jesus Christ.**

99. **You must be a soul winner to fulfil Isaiah's prophecies on God's efforts to save the lost.**

> **"Now therefore, what do I have here," declares the LORD, "seeing that My people have been taken away without cause?" Again the LORD declares, "Those who rule over them howl, and My name is continually blasphemed all day long.**
> **"Therefore My people shall know My name; therefore in that day I am the one who is speaking, "Here I am.'"**
> **How lovely on the mountains Are the feet of him who brings good news, Who announces peace And brings good news of happiness, who announces salvation, and says to Zion, "Your God reigns!"**
> **Listen! Your watchmen lift up their voices, they shout joyfully together; for they will see with their own eyes When the LORD restores Zion.**
> **Break forth, shout joyfully together, you waste places of Jerusalem; for the LORD has comforted His people, He has redeemed Jerusalem.**
> **The LORD has bared His holy arm in the sight of all the nations, That all the ends of the earth may see the salvation of our God.**
> **Isaiah 52:5-10, NASB**

100. **You must be a soul winner because God demonstrated His love towards us when we were sinners and we must also demonstrate our love to the unsaved.**

> *"Missionary zeal does not grow out of intellectual beliefs nor out of theological arguments, but out of love."*
> *Roland Allen*

But God commendeth his love toward us, in that, while we were yet sinners, Christ died for us.

Romans 5:8

101. You must be a soul winner because we must by all means save some.

To the weak became I as weak, that I might gain the weak: I am made all things to all men, that I might by all means save some.

1 Corinthians 9:22

102. You must be a soul winner because Jesus said we must be about our Father's business.

And he said unto them, How is it that ye sought me? wist ye not that I must be about my Father's business?

Luke 2:49

103. You must be a soul winner because apostle Peter said there is salvation in no other name but Jesus Christ.

Neither is there salvation in any other: for there is none other name under heaven given among men, whereby we must be saved.

Acts 4:12

104. You must be a soul winner because the Gospel offers the greatest of everything.

For God so loved the world, that he gave his only begotten Son, that whosoever believeth in him should not perish, but have everlasting life.

John 3:16

i. The Gospel offers the greatest invitation ever.
ii. The Gospel offers the love of the greatest person.
iii. The Gospel offers the greatest kind of love.
iv. The Gospel offers salvation to the greatest number of people.

v. The Gospel offers the greatest gift to man…eternal life.

vi. The Gospel offers everyone the chance to do the greatest human act - to believe in Christ is the greatest act of a human being.

vii.The Gospel offers the greatest escape from judgement and Hell.

viii. The Gospel offers the greatest destination - Heaven.

105. You must be a soul winner because there is no greater love than this.

a. Jesus' love is greater than a man's love for women.

I am distressed for thee, my brother Jonathan: very pleasant hast thou been unto me: thy love to me was wonderful, passing the love of women.

2 Samuel 1:26

And Jacob loved Rachel; and said, I will serve thee seven years for Rachel thy younger daughter.

Genesis 29:18

b. Jesus' love is greater than a man's love for his nation.

And when they came to Jesus, they besought him instantly, saying, That he was worthy for whom he should do this: For he loveth our nation, and he hath built us a synagogue.

Luke 7:4-5

106. You must be a soul winner because Hell is a frightening place that awaits the souls of lost and rebellious sinners.

a. Hell is a place of sorrows.

The sorrows of hell compassed me about; the snares of death prevented me;

2 Samuel 22:6

b. Hell is a place where you never die.

And if thy hand offend thee, cut it off: it is better for thee to enter into life maimed, than having two

hands to go into hell, into the fire that never shall be quenched: Where their worm dieth not, and the fire is not quenched.

Mark 9:43-44

c. Hell is a place worth giving your eyes, arms and legs in order to avoid.

And if thy hand offend thee, cut it off: it is better for thee to enter into life maimed, than having two hands to go into hell, into the fire that never shall be quenched: Where their worm dieth not, and the fire is not quenched.

And if thy foot offend thee, cut it off: it is better for thee to enter halt into life, than having two feet to be cast into hell, into the fire that never shall be quenched: Where their worm dieth not, and the fire is not quenched.

And if thine eye offend thee, pluck it out: it is better for thee to enter into the kingdom of God with one eye, than having two eyes to be cast into hell fire:

Mark 9:43-47

d. Hell is a place that is constantly being expanded to receive more people.

Therefore hell hath enlarged herself, and opened her mouth without measure: and their glory, and their multitude, and their pomp, and he that rejoiceth, shall descend into it.

Isaiah 5:14

e. Hell is a place where you will be welcomed by demons and dead people.

Hell from beneath is moved for thee to meet thee at thy coming: it stirreth up the dead for thee...

Isaiah 14:9

f. Hell is a place where people beg for a drop of water.

There was a certain rich man, which was clothed in purple and fine linen, and fared sumptuously every

day: and there was a certain beggar named Lazarus, which was laid at his gate, full of sores,
And desiring to be fed with the crumbs which fell from the rich man's table: moreover the dogs came and licked his sores.
And it came to pass, that the beggar died, and was carried by the angels into Abraham's bosom: the rich man also died, and was buried; and in hell he lift up his eyes, being in torments, and seeth Abraham afar off, and Lazarus in his bosom.
And he cried and said, Father Abraham, have mercy on me, and send Lazarus, that he may dip the tip of his finger in water, and cool my tongue; for I am tormented in this flame.

Luke 16:19-24

g. Hell is a frightening place of darkness and chains.

For if God spared not the angels that sinned, but cast them down to hell, and delivered them into chains of darkness, to be reserved unto judgment;

2 Peter 2:4

h. Hell is a vast burning lake of fire.

And the beast was taken, and with him the false prophet that wrought miracles before him, with which he deceived them that had received the mark of the beast, and them that worshipped his image. These both were cast alive into a lake of fire burning with brimstone.

Revelation 19:20

i. Hell is a vast lake of burning sulphur (a chemical element similar to oxygen).

And the devil that deceived them was cast into the lake of fire and brimstone (burning sulphur), where the beast and the false prophet are, and shall be tormented day and night for ever and ever.

Revelation 20:10

j. Hell is a place that is never full. There is space for you there if you stubbornly refuse Gospel salvation through Christ.

Hell and destruction are never full; so the eyes of man are never satisfied.

Proverbs 27:20

107. You must be a soul winner because the whole world is thirsty and searching for the water that satisfies.

In the last day, that great day of the feast, Jesus stood and cried, saying, If any man thirst, let him come unto me, and drink. He that believeth on me, as the scripture hath said, out of his belly shall flow rivers of living water.
But this spake he of the Spirit, which they that believe on him should receive: for the Holy Ghost was not yet given; because that Jesus was not yet glorified.) Many of the people therefore, when they heard this saying, said, Of a truth this is the Prophet.

John 7:37-40

But whosoever drinketh of the water that I shall give him shall never thirst; but the water that I shall give him shall be in him a well of water springing up into everlasting life.

John 4:14

a. Is anyone thirsty? Yes, we are all thirsty. Men are always seeking to quench their thirst in the wrong way.

b. Men try to quench their thirst with money.

Wilt thou set thine eyes upon that which is not? for riches certainly make themselves wings; they fly away as an eagle toward heaven.

Proverbs 23:5

c. Men try to quench their thirst by seeking the unknown and seeking knowledge.

Ever learning, and never able to come to the knowledge
of the truth.

2 Timothy 3:7

For in much wisdom is much grief: and he that
increaseth knowledge increaseth sorrow.

Ecclesiastes 1:18

And further, by these, my son, be admonished: of
making many books there is no end; and much study
is a weariness of the flesh.

Ecclesiastes 12:12

d. Men try to quench their thirst by seeking pleasure.

For the time past of our life may suffice us to have
wrought the will of the Gentiles, when we walked
in lasciviousness, lusts, excess of wine, revellings,
banquetings, and abominable idolatries: Wherein
they think it strange that ye run not with them to the
same excess of riot, speaking evil of you:

1 Peter 4:3-4

e. Men try to quench their thirst through alcohol.

Who hath woe? who hath sorrow? who hath
contentions? who hath babbling? who hath wounds
without cause? who hath redness of eyes?
They that tarry long at the wine; they that go to seek
mixed wine.
Look not thou upon the wine when it is red, when
it giveth his colour in the cup, when it moveth itself
aright.

Proverbs 23:29-31

Woe unto them that rise up early in the morning,
that they may follow strong drink; that continue until
night, till wine inflame them!

Isaiah 5:11

f. Men try to quench their thirst with sex.

Let not thine heart decline to her ways, go not astray in her paths. For she hath cast down many wounded: yea, many strong men have been slain by her. Her house is the way to hell, going down to the chambers of death.

Proverbs 7:25-27

g. Men try to quench their thirst through homosexuality.

The shew of their countenance doth witness against them; and they declare their sin as Sodom, they hide it not. Woe unto their soul! for they have rewarded evil unto themselves.

Isaiah 3:9

Behold, this was the iniquity of thy sister Sodom, pride, fulness of bread, and abundance of idleness was in her and in her daughters, neither did she strengthen the hand of the poor and needy.

Ezekiel 16:49

h. Men try to quench their thirst by working and working and working.

There is one alone, and there is not a second; yea, he hath neither child nor brother: yet is there no end of all his labour; neither is his eye satisfied with riches; neither saith he, For whom do I labour, and bereave my soul of good? This is also vanity, yea, it is a sore travail.

Ecclesiastes 4:8

i. Only Christ can quench the thirst and the search.

And Jesus said unto them, I am the bread of life: he that cometh to me shall never hunger; and he that believeth on me shall never thirst.

John 6:35

108. You must be a soul winner because God has sent us to invite people to the feast of the Lord.

And the lord said unto the servant, Go out into the highways and hedges, and compel them to come in, that my house may be filled.

Luke 14:23

a. God is inviting you to come to Him. Throughout the Bible, God invites people to come to Him.

Come, and let us return unto the LORD: for he hath torn, and he will heal us; he hath smitten, and he will bind us up.

Hosea 6:1

Behold, I stand at the door, and knock: if any man hear my voice, and open the door, I will come in to him, and will sup with him, and he with me.

Revelation 3:20

I have sent also unto you all my servants the prophets, rising up early and sending them, saying, return ye now every man from his evil way, and amend your doings, and go not after other gods to serve them, and ye shall dwell in the land which I have given to you and to your fathers: but ye have not inclined your ear, nor hearkened unto me.

Jeremiah 35:15

Say unto them, As I live, saith the Lord GOD, I have no pleasure in the death of the wicked; but that the wicked turn from his way and live: turn ye, turn ye from your evil ways; for why will ye die, O house of Israel?

Ezekiel 33:11

b. Little things and little excuses keep people away from God.

Yet a little sleep, a little slumber, a little folding of the hands to sleep: So shall thy poverty come as one that travelleth; and thy want as an armed man.

Proverbs 24:33-34

c. Your land, your property and your business must not keep you away from God.

And take heed to yourselves, lest at any time your hearts be overcharged with surfeiting, and drunkenness, and cares of this life, and so that day come upon you unawares.

Luke 21:34

d. Even your family must not keep you away from God.

If any man come to me, and hate not his father, and mother, and wife, and children, and brethren, and sisters, yea, and his own life also, he cannot be my disciple.

Luke 14:26

And he said unto another, Follow me. But he said, Lord, suffer me first to go and bury my father.

Luke 9:59

e. Unfortunately, many reject the great invitation. Therefore, poor and unfortunate people will fill the places in Heaven.

Nevertheless, if thou warn the wicked of his way to turn from it; if he do not turn from his way, he shall die in his iniquity; but thou hast delivered thy soul.

Ezekiel 33:9

f. It is a dangerous mistake to reject the invitation and the love of God.

How shall we escape, if we neglect so great salvation; which at the first began to be spoken by the Lord, and was confirmed unto us by them that heard him;

Hebrews 2:3

See that ye refuse not him that speaketh. For if they escaped not who refused him that spake on earth, much more shall not we escape, if we turn away from him that speaketh from heaven:

Hebrews 12:25

g. At the great feast, you will enjoy the bread - the bread of life.

This is the bread which cometh down from heaven, that a man may eat thereof, and not die.

I am the living bread which came down from heaven: if any man eat of this bread, he shall live for ever: and the bread that I will give is my flesh, which I will give for the life of the world.

John 6:50-51

h. At the great feast, you will enjoy the milk.

As newborn babes, desire the sincere milk of the word, that ye may grow thereby:

1 Peter 2:2

i. At the great feast, you will enjoy the meat.

But strong meat belongeth to them that are of full age, even those who by reason of use have their senses exercised to discern both good and evil.

Hebrews 5:14

j. At the great feast, you will enjoy the water of the Word and the Holy Spirit.

But whosoever drinketh of the water that I shall give him shall never thirst; but the water that I shall give him shall be in him a well of water springing up into everlasting life.

John 4:14

And the Spirit and the bride say, Come. And let him that heareth say, Come. And let him that is athirst come. And whosoever will, let him take the water of life freely.

Revelation 22:17

k. At the great feast, you will enjoy the fruits.

But the fruit of the Spirit is love, joy, peace, longsuffering, gentleness, goodness, faith, Meekness, temperance: against such there is no law.

Galatians 5:22-23

l. At the great feast, you will enjoy the wine - the blood of Jesus.

And he took the cup, and gave thanks, and gave it to them, saying, Drink ye all of it; For this is my blood of the new testament, which is shed for many for the remission of sins.

Matthew 26:27-28

109. **You must be a soul winner because people are wasting their lives away without Jesus.**

And when he had spent all, there arose a mighty famine in that land; and he began to be in want.

Luke 15:14

110. **You must be a soul winner to give other people a chance to become new creatures. When people are saved, they become new creatures and they are regenerated.**

Therefore if any man be in Christ, he is a new creature: old things are passed away; behold, all things are become new.

2 Corinthians 5:17

Not by works of righteousness which we have done, but according to his mercy he saved us, by the washing of regeneration, and renewing of the Holy Ghost;

Titus 3:5

111. **You must be a soul winner so that the sins of mankind can be purged by the blood of Jesus Christ.**

> And almost all things are by the law purged with blood; and without shedding of blood is no remission.
>
> **Hebrews 9:22**

112. You must be a soul winner because we need to be reconciled to Jesus Christ.

To be reconciled speaks of re-uniting you with your God. The whole world needs to be reunited with God. That is why we must be soul winners.

> **Being justified freely by his grace through the redemption that is in Christ Jesus:**
>
> **Romans 3:24**

113. You must be a soul winner so that people can have peace with God through the blood of Jesus.

> **And, having made peace through the blood of his cross, by him to reconcile all things unto himself; by him, I say, whether they be things in earth, or things in heaven.**
>
> **Colossians 1:20**

114. You must be a soul winner because people need to be redeemed (bought back) from the devil. To be redeemed means to be bought back from the grips of Satan. Your salvation is a legal acquisition that the enemy cannot dispute.

> **And they sung a new song, saying, Thou art worthy to take the book, and to open the seals thereof: for thou wast slain, and hast redeemed us to God by thy blood out of every kindred, and tongue, and people, and nation;**
>
> **Revelation 5:9**

> **Forasmuch as ye know that ye were not redeemed with corruptible things, as silver and gold, from your vain conversation received by tradition from your fathers;**

But with the precious blood of Christ, as of a lamb without blemish and without spot:

1 Peter 1:18-19

115. You must be a soul winner because today is the day of salvation.

There is no better time to be saved than right now. No one can guarantee tomorrow. You can only guarantee right now. Everyone must have the opportunity for salvation today.

Again, he limiteth a certain day, saying in David, to day, after so long a time; as it is said, to day if ye will hear his voice, harden not your hearts.

Hebrews 4:7

116. You must be a soul winner because we cannot escape if we neglect this great salvation.

No greater way of escape can be provided. It is the way out for the whole world. We must be soul winners because everybody's got to know about this great way of salvation.

How shall we escape, if we neglect so great salvation; which at the first began to be spoken by the Lord, and was confirmed unto us by them that heard him;

Hebrews 2:3

117. You must be a soul winner because one day we will rejoice over the soul winning seeds that we have sown!

Every time we preach the Gospel, we are sowing seeds of salvation. One day, we will see the fruits of soul winning and be glad that we were soul winners.

He that goeth forth and weepeth, bearing precious seed, shall doubtless come again with rejoicing, bringing his sheaves with him.

Psalms 126:6

118. You must be a soul winner because there is only one way to get to Heaven.

a. There is a way that seems right unto man; these are the ways of men.

There is a way which seemeth right unto a man, but the end thereof are the ways of death.

Proverbs 14:12

b. The way of hard work is not the way to Heaven or to God.

There is one alone, and there is not a second; yea, he hath neither child nor brother: yet is there no end of all his labour; neither is his eye satisfied with riches; neither saith he, For whom do I labour, and bereave my soul of good? This is also vanity, yea, it is a sore travail.

Ecclesiastes 4:8

c. A life of pleasure is not the way to Heaven or to God.

Therefore hear now this, thou that art given to pleasures, that dwellest carelessly, that sayest in thine heart, I am, and none else beside me; I shall not sit as a widow, neither shall I know the loss of children:
But these two things shall come to thee in a moment in one day, the loss of children, and widowhood: they shall come upon thee in their perfection for the multitude of thy sorceries, and for the great abundance of thine enchantments.

Isaiah 47:8-9

d. Occultism is not the way to Heaven or to God.

There shall not be found among you any one that maketh his son or his daughter to pass through the fire, or that useth divination, or an observer of times, or an enchanter, or a witch,

Deuteronomy 18:10

e. Worshipping idols is not the way to Heaven.

Ye shall make you no idols nor graven image, neither rear you up a standing image, neither shall ye set up any image of stone in your land, to bow down unto it: for I am the LORD your God.

Leviticus 26:1

Thou shalt not make unto thee any graven image, or any likeness of any thing that is in heaven above, or that is in the earth beneath, or that is in the water under the earth:

Exodus 20:4

Take heed to yourselves, that your heart be not deceived, and ye turn aside, and serve other gods, and worship them;

Deuteronomy 11:16

They shall be turned back, they shall be greatly ashamed, that trust in graven images, that say to the molten images, Ye are our gods.

Isaiah 42:17

f. Being religious is not the way to Heaven. Following traditions, singing hymns without knowing God is not the way to Heaven.

This people draweth nigh unto me with their mouth, and honoureth me with their lips; but their heart is far from me.

Matthew 15:8

g. Achieving money and fame is not the way to Heaven.

Riches profit not in the day of wrath: but righteousness delivereth from death. The righteousness of the perfect shall direct his way: but the wicked shall fall by his own wickedness.

Proverbs 11:4-5

h. Following any other religion is not the way to Heaven. False religions offer many other ways that are not true.

For there is one God, and one mediator between God and men, the man Christ Jesus;

1 Timothy 2:5

Neither is there salvation in any other: for there is none other name under heaven given among men, whereby we must be saved.

Acts 4:12

i. Being a good person and doing good works is not the way. Good works will not take you to Heaven. The only way is through the blood of Jesus! There is a life that seems to be the life, but Jesus Christ is the life - He gives abundant life.

But we are all as an unclean thing, and all our righteousnesses are as filthy rags; and we all do fade as a leaf; and our iniquities, like the wind, have taken us away.

Isaiah 64:6

As it is written, There is none righteous, no, not one.

Romans 3:10

j. No one, including you, comes to the Father except through Jesus. "No one" means presidents, your mother, friends, your brothers, your teachers - come to Jesus today, come to the cross, and come to the blood!

Jesus saith unto him, I am the way, the truth, and the life: no man cometh unto the Father but by me.

John 14:6

119. **You must be a soul winner because *Mendel Taylor* said, "The church must send, or it will end."**

120. **You must be a soul winner because you now have MORE THAN ENOUGH REASONS to be a soul winner!!!**

CHAPTER 2

Missionaries and the Example of the Basel Mission

GO YE therefore, and teach ALL NATIONS, baptizing them in the name of the Father, and of the Son, and of the Holy Ghost:

Teaching them to observe all things whatsoever I have commanded you: And, lo, I am with you alway, even unto the end of the world. Amen.

Matthew 28:19,20

This is the famous Great Commission that compels Christians to go into all the world as preachers. Unfortunately, it is one of the least obeyed commands of the Bible. The Church tends to "stay" more than to "go". These were the last words of Jesus and must therefore be taken very seriously.

This command is as valid today as it was two thousand years ago. It is not only the promises of prosperity that are valid today. The instruction to "go into all the world" still rings loud and clear as an eternal command from the Lord.

This command takes on a new meaning when you think of the kind of world we live in today. The regions where Christianity used to be active have now changed. The spiritually alive sections of the world have shifted from Europe to the poorer and more deprived parts of the world. Today, Europe is the seat of Satan, with most people on that continent being atheists or non-believers. There is now a great need for us to reach out to such parts of the world.

The Shifting Responsibility

It looks as though the responsibility of spreading the Gospel has shifted from Whites to men of colour. Whenever we think of missionaries we think of White people coming to save the unreached and uncivilised Black races. We imagine pious White missionaries going through the sweltering tropical jungles to reach savages in remote villages.

However, all this has changed! There are not as many savages in remote villages as there were four hundred years ago. Today, it is the White people who have turned into pagans and infidels. It is the White people living in rich and affluent cities who have no knowledge of God.

Do not misunderstand me, there are still thousands of poor villages and towns which need to hear about Jesus. But no one can deny the fact that the spiritual landscape of the world has changed enormously. The cloud of ignorance and spiritual backwardness has shifted to the western nations of the world.

Spiritual death has placed its icy hands on the churches of Europe. Church buildings that seated hundreds of ardent worshippers every Sunday, today receive less than fifteen old men and women.

Many churches meet every other week instead of every week. On Sunday mornings, the young people are recovering from hangovers and the debauchery of the night before. They have no time for or knowledge of God.

In Switzerland for instance, many of the pastors do not believe in God. They are often state employees who have a job to do.

A recent millennium survey in England showed that only 28% of the population believed in the traditional understanding of a "personal God". 37% in the survey saw God as a "spirit or life force". This obviously shows a lack of knowledge of the Bible and its teachings.

There was also a remarkable drop in the number of people who believed in Jesus as the Son of God. 45% of those questioned believed that Jesus was the Son of God as compared to 71% in 1957. This shows that over the last forty years, over one third of the believers have given up their faith.

And because iniquity shall abound, THE LOVE OF MANY SHALL WAX COLD.
Matthew 24:12

It is time for us to go again into every corner of the world with the Good News of Jesus Christ. I am very grateful for the Americans and Europeans who came to Africa with the Gospel. Perhaps I would belong to some other religion today, if they had not come.

This command must be taken seriously today. If we do not go when He has told us to, God may be forced to use other methods to drive us into the mission fields.

In Acts 1:8, Jesus told His disciples to wait for the Spirit. He promised that after the Holy Spirit came, they would be able to go very far with the Gospel. Unfortunately, like most of us do, the disciples did not obey the commandment but stayed together in the comfort of Jerusalem.

> **But ye shall receive power, after that the Holy Ghost is come upon you: and ye shall be witnesses unto me both in Jerusalem, and in all Judaea, and in Samaria, and unto the uttermost part of the earth.**
>
> **Acts 1:8**

It is much easier to change the carpet in the church and to have a church picnic than to go into all the world and preach. It is when you do what is hard and difficult that you move forward in the right direction. It may not be easy, but it is worth it!

When the Church failed to send out missionaries, the Lord allowed persecution to speak a little louder about missionary work.

> **...And at that time there was A GREAT PERSECUTION against the church which was at Jerusalem; and they were all SCATTERED ABROAD throughout the regions of Judaea and Samaria, except the apostles.**
> **Then Philip went down to the city of Samaria, and preached Christ unto them.**
> **And the people with one accord gave heed unto those things which Philip spake, hearing and seeing the miracles which he did.**
> **For unclean spirits, crying with loud voice, came out of many that were possessed with them: and many taken with palsies, and that were lame, were healed.**
> **And there was great joy in that city.**
>
> **Acts 8:1, 5-8**

Can you see what power lay within the disciples who were gathered together in Jerusalem? They just had to go! When they went, great things happened. You have no idea what will happen when you go. I speak to all pastors and men of authority in the Church. It is your duty to send men and women as missionaries into the entire world. **If you fail to do this, you are inadvertently sentencing those parts of the world to spiritual death and Hell.**

I shudder when I imagine what it would have been like if missionaries had not sacrificed their lives for some of us to know Jesus. It is this very thought that spurs me on in my quest for world evangelism. I know that within me lies the power to teach whole nations. Jesus said we should go to the world and teach nations. By your obedience, multitudes will find peace and salvation. I think we often do not know the effect of one man's obedience.

> **Therefore as by the offence of one judgment came upon all men to condemnation; even so BY THE RIGHTEOUSNESS OF ONE THE FREE GIFT CAME UPON ALL MEN...**
>
> **Romans 5:18**

The Basel Mission

The story of the Basel Mission of Switzerland has always intrigued me. Perhaps it is because my grandparents and mother come from there. I have always been touched by the sacrifice that the Basel missionaries made for the advancement of the Gospel in Ghana.

Is There No Need for Missionaries?

Some people thought there was no need for such an organisation to send missionaries into the world when Swiss people themselves needed Christ. This is a common argument that leads to "paralysis by analysis".

I know there are people today who would say, "Why should we send missionaries to any country when there are millions of unsaved people all around in our own country?" "There is no need to go anywhere; the sinners are next door!" "It is much more economical to do evangelism in our neighbourhood!" As I said earlier, I shudder when I think of what would have happened if that argument had prevailed over the simple command of our Lord to "go".

I wish to quote the argument that one such person made against the concept of missionaries being sent out from Switzerland in the nineteenth century:

> *"Wouldn't it be strange, if a mission were sent out from Switzerland, while there is such dire need that someone comes to us in order to put an end to the rampant domestic paganism in the heads of our own nobles and commoners, smart-heads and dimwits alike?"* (Excerpt translated from Schlatter, Vol. 1, p.13).

It seems there was a loaded debate as to whether people should be sent out into the mission fields of the world or not. However, some zealous members who would not be deterred, set up the *Basel Evangelical Missionary Society*. Gradually a complete missionary organisation, with its own overseas programmes was established.

Into All the World

You will notice from this history, that the Swiss people attempted to go "into all the world". They were not distracted by the fact that there were sinners in their own cities. **Jesus never said that we should go when everyone around us is saved. He just said that we should go!** Notice how the Church in Switzerland sent missionaries to all parts of the world at great cost. They sent people to Russia, West Africa and Asia.

One thousand eight hundred years after Christ had given His instruction, there was a need to obey and go into all the world! Today, two thousand years after Jesus gave the missionary command, I declare to you that there is still a need for us to go! We must go! If we love Him, we must feed His sheep! We must find a way of going to every single nation of this world with the Gospel of Jesus Christ.

The example of the missionaries of old should serve as inspiration to us in this modern world. We must not just say, "Wow, that was a great effort!" We must rise up and do the same and more!

Let's now see how the Basel Missionaries gave up their lives as they obeyed the Great Commission.

The Basel Missionaries in Russia

[1]In 1820, two graduates were sent out to the Caucasus - an area that had been newly annexed by the Tsarist Russian empire. In these vast lands, between the Black Sea and the Caspian, there were sizeable communities of German and Swiss settlers in need of pastoral care. But there were also the hitherto little known indigenous peoples. Some of them, had already been Christianised in the early beginnings of the faith whilst others had become Muslims.

It was particularly this latter group whom the Basel Missionaries tried to reach with the Gospel. However, this effort ended when the Tsar, faced with a revolt, removed the missionaries out of his empire.

The Basel Mission continued to despatch missionaries to the world through other missionary societies. The feedback from these outreaches opened the eyes of their leadership to new missionary horizons. Notably, West Africa, India and China. These destinations eventually became the most important targets of the Basel Mission's activities.

It wasn't easy and they certainly had problems. Arguments over hierarchic subordination, questions of liturgy and issues of culture arose. However, the work progressed and other people followed the Basel Mission idea and the Bremen Mission for example, was established.

The Basel Missionaries in Sierra Leone

The first targets of the Basel Mission in Sub-Sahara Africa were Sierra Leone and Liberia.

These territories had been acquired by British and American philanthropists respectively with the intention to resettle freed slaves. Governmental backing had been assured in both cases. In Basel, this development was seen as a good chance for gaining a missionary foothold on the little known African Continent. News went around that a modern education system was about to be set up. Hence, teachers and pastoral workers were required.

According to the thinking of the European missionary movement of that time, the "Whiteman" had to repay an enormous moral debt because of his former trade in slaves. This debt could be repaid through good works. Another aspect was that some indigenous societies still persisted in hunting and selling their next of kin; they had to be freed from such conditions of moral backwardness.

"Sierra Leone" was originally the only name of the peninsula, on which the modern capital of Freetown is located. Freetown itself was founded in 1787. The ex-slaves to be resettled came from England and North America, later also from intercepted ships in the Atlantic Ocean. At that time, the hinterland of the peninsula appeared on the maps of the Europeans as nameless tribal territory.

It was precisely in this part of the country, where the Basel men ultimately wanted to work: away from the European influenced coastal settlements. In January 1823, four missionaries arrived in Freetown, from where they ventured out to their individual destinations up-country. Two of the "brothers" were accompanied by their wives. A few months later, the bachelors and the wives of the two remaining missionaries died of yellow fever, which had broken out in epidemic proportions. In no time, most of the expatriate community were dead or gone.

The remaining "brothers" and a missionary, who had arrived later, stayed back as the only Europeans in the territory. They returned to Freetown to carry on the work of the British-based Church Mission Society, under whose protection they had come. A year later, the colonial administration decreed that henceforth only British nationals would be allowed in for doing missionary work. At this stage, the Committee in Basel decided to shift its focus to Liberia.

The Basel Missionaries in Liberia

The territory of Liberia had been dedicated as a resettlement area in 1817 by the African Colonial Society. This private organisation constituted itself in Washington, where it enjoyed governmental backing. The Society's leader, an American citizen by name of Jehudi Ashmun, was installed as the territory's first Governor. Liberia should henceforth be developed as a homeland for freed slaves from plantations in the Southern United States.

In 1847, it became sub-Saharan Africa's first independent country. As can be imagined, the setting up of an American-type administration on these shores was by no means easy. At one stage in 1822, three dozens of the new colonists had to fight back about 800 natives.

But a few years later, Ashmun felt comfortable enough to issue a public announcement that invited missionary societies to start work in Liberia. The call fell on ready ears in Basel. After the setback experienced in Sierra Leone it offered fresh hope.

Anxieties concerning the high health risks were brushed off with the typical confidence of those, who lay their ultimate trust in the hands of "Him who had called them". Inspector Blumhardt wrote in the Mission Magazine of 1827: ***"We would have considered it shameful to the name of Christ to close our hearts and ears to the misery and the outcries for help of these poor souls in Africa, just because we shied away from the dangers of death. Neither does the European slave trader shy away from the perils of a life-consuming climate, when he roams the same shores day and night like a predator..."***

As it turned out, Ashmun had painted a rather rosy picture in which *"reality and wishful thinking were inextricably mixed up"*. Adequate housing was unavailable even in the capital; living costs prohibitively high and, worst of all, the population showed little interest in what the missionaries had to offer. The Governor himself fell seriously ill after the arrival of four Basel Mission missionaries in 1828. He soon had to be repatriated to the United States, where he died three months later.

The remaining administrators did not really care about the missionary endeavour. Someone seemed to have even retained the mail coming from Basel instead of passing it on. But the proverbial "straw that broke the camel's back" came in the guise of the hostile attitude of the American Baptist community, then the only other church organisation in Monrovia.

These fellow Christians reportedly deemed it necessary to exclude the Basel "brothers" from church service, for the sole reason that they had not been baptised in accordance with Baptist rules! This rendered the newcomers ineffective as preachers, since they had lost all credibility in the eyes of the town folks.

Disgusted, the missionaries left Monrovia to set up their stations inland, just as their colleagues had previously done in Sierra Leone. They all went their own way, in order to work among the native population. Bit by bit, the group dwindled again due to death or illness.

Finally, the last remaining missionary's seed money ran out, before he had managed to establish a viable economic basis as expected by the leadership in Basel.

After this fiasco, the Mission Directors decided to place the next investment on more promising soil. **This opened the way for the most successful chapter of Basel missionary activities in Africa: the one on the Gold Coast.** But other important ventures on the Black Continent were to follow, foremost in Nigeria, Cameroon, Congo and the Sudan.[1]

Lessons from the Basel Mission

There are two important lessons to learn from the mission to Liberia.

■ **Missionaries had to become farmers, traders and builders in order to survive as missionaries in a foreign country.**

The missionaries were expected to establish a "viable economic basis". This meant that they were to find jobs that would sustain them in ministry. This is the lay ministry in practice in the nineteenth century.

You can readily see that it is not a new idea to let people work for a living as they do the work of ministry. I am constantly amazed that people want the church to bear an impossible financial burden that limits the scope and extent of its outreach work.

Today, people take pride in announcing how many hundreds of people the church employs. It is as though the more people you have on your payroll, the more successful you are. Dear friend, what matters is what we are able to accomplish for the Lord. We must win the lost at any cost! If it means we have to find a job, so be it. If it means we have to be fully employed by the church, so be it!

■ **If European slave traders were prepared to risk their lives and health roaming the shores of tropical West Africa for money, then the Christian missionaries could risk their lives for the souls of men.**

We must learn from the attitude of Inspector Blumhardt who thought it was a shame to close our ears to the cries of souls. His logic was very simple.

The Basel Missionaries in Ghana

[1]Around 1826, the Basel Mission sought to widen its network of sponsors. Like-minded religious circles were approached,

particularly in Scandinavia. These advances from Basel were first picked up in Denmark by Pastor Rönne, the Inspector of the Danish Missionary Society (DMS).

Rönne had once been a tutor of the Crown Prince and enjoyed the confidence of the Danish Court. He also was eager to give the DMS a new push, as it was about to slip into a state of lethargy. An arrangement with the dynamic Basel Mission seemed to be just the right approach.

Precisely in that same year, Governor Johan von Richelieu, the Governor of the Danish station of Christiansborg on the Gold Coast (Danish sources refer to it as the "Guinea Coast"), arrived in Copenhagen on home leave. *While briefing the King, von Richelieu impressed on His Majesty the urgent need for teachers and preachers in this Danish possession.*

Like the other European powers, who had established themselves on the Gold Coast, Denmark pursued essentially commercial interests. Besides trading with the indigenous population and keeping invaders away from the surrounding areas, the Danish garrison exercised very little influence over the territory.

The fort of Christiansborg with its Danish and mulatto population was virtually an European enclave on African soil. Seen through the eyes of its expatriate staff, a term on the Gold Coast meant privations and restrictions in many ways. Moreover, it bore a high risk of death through tropical diseases. A man would go there only for filling his pocket as fast as possible, usually by bartering guns and schnapps for gold and slaves.

Under the prevailing Danish law, each colonial employee was allowed to co-habit with one native woman, who thereby acquired certain rights and privileges. This gave rise to a steadily growing mulatto population. It was for the educational and spiritual needs of these people, and of course for the benefit of the Danish garrison staff, that the Danish Government had invited the Basel missionaries to establish themselves in Christiansborg.

In Basel, one had a different outlook. By missionary standards, which were notoriously strict, the level of morality at Christiansborg appeared as abysmal. The Mission Committee showed little enthusiasm for the idea of uplifting the new and so far unsettled class of people that resulted from the promiscuity of European soldiers.

In any case, the focus of the Basel missionaries was on the indigenous population, not the Europeans and their affiliations. But they were ready for a compromise, i.e. to let one of their staff serve the garrison, while the others would eventually be despatched to areas outside.

An agreement was finally reached, for which both sides made concessions. The Basel Mission got the permission for inland work and in return accepted the hierarchic subordination of its missionaries under a Danish Lutheran Bishop. Otherwise they could retain full operational autonomy.

In December 1828, four missionaries arrived at Christiansborg. They were the Germans Karl F. Salbach, Gottlieb Holzwarth and Johannes Henke, and the Swiss Johannes Schmidt. Death cruelly intervened. Within a few months three of them had already perished. Towards the end of 1831 the fourth one, Henke, also followed them into the grave.

Had it not been for the slow pace of communications in the 19th century, the Mission Committee would probably have given up the whole idea. **However, before the news of the last death arrived at headquarters, the Mission Board had already decided to send reinforcements.**

In 1832 these arrived: Andreas Riis and Peter Jäger, both from Denmark, and Christian Friedrich Heinze, a medical doctor from Saxony. Dr Heinze was to study the situation of the extraordinary health risks that would be encountered on the Gold Coast, and come out with recommendations for preventive measures. Ironically, "Invincible Death" summoned him first. And not long after this loss, Riis lowered Jäger into the grave. *He nearly followed himself, had it not been for a native herbalist, who saw Riis through the worst convulsions.* An Afro-Danish trader, George Lutterodt, then offered Riis his comfortable farmhouse for recovery.

In 1835, Riis started building-up the Basel Mission's first inland station on the Gold Coast. It was in the town of Akropong, capital of the small Akuapem State. Riis erected his living quarters first. The house was put on a solid stone foundation and equipped with doors, windows and a functional wide roof.

Such attributes the local people had never seen before. His energetic way of taking action earned Riis the nickname of "Osiadan", meaning the house builder (chapter 3.3.). The missionaries that followed produced similar structures. Quite a few of these can be seen to this day.

Akropong eventually became the very nerve centre of the Basel Mission in Ghana. Symbolically speaking: Riis' stone-based house in Akropong had served as *"the rock on which the Basel Church was built"!*

Why did Riis choose Akropong for establishing his first inland mission station? For answering this question we shall now briefly turn to the second half of the previous, 18th century.

There we discover another remarkable pioneer: the Danish citizen Dr P.E. Isert, a botanist and medical doctor, also an admirer of the Genevan philosopher Jean-Jacques Rousseau. Influenced by the latter's "back-to-nature philosophy", Isert was convinced that the damage done to African societies during the period of the transatlantic slave trade could be somewhat repaired, if one encouraged and assisted Africans in the running of their own *"plantation colonies"* on indigenous soil. These lands would be reserved for ex-slaves, who were to make a living out of crops produced for overseas markets. *The concept we see emerging here could in fact be the very first development project ever proposed for Africa!*

Isert mooted his idea in a widely sold book after he returned from an exploratory journey to the Gold Coast in 1786. For the same purpose, he later returned to the Gold Coast where he explored the plateau on the Akuapem range, about 60-km inland from Christiansborg. **He wrote in his memoirs that he literally had to cut his way through the bush, crossing 40 km of the Akra Plain.** On the plateau, he encountered a comparatively healthy and hospitable environment.

In any case, Nana Atiemo, the Paramount Chief of the State of Akuapem at the time, readily granted him land. The project seemed to take off well. A first report dated 16 January 1789, was carried by Isert himself to Christiansborg. As it turned out, this was also his last one, since he suddenly succumbed to a fever. After a few years, however, the project had to be abandoned. Nevertheless, Dr Isert's efforts were not wasted. They inspired the Basel missionaries, who arrived on the Gold Coast half a century later.

When the Basel missionaries first set foot on the Gold Coast in 1828, the territory - which later became the Republic of Ghana - had British, Danish and Dutch settlements interspersed along its shores.

These settlements were essentially fortified trading posts from which the respective governors exercised some indirect control over limited tracts of land extending not too far into the densely forested coastal belt. Various kings, among whom the leader of the Asantes, the Asantehene, the most powerful, held the remainder of the territory.

Throughout the 19th century, the Asante Kingdom fiercely resisted any European attempts at further colonisation. Only after the British had bought up the Danish and Dutch possessions, and henceforth could launch a cohesive campaign against the Asantes, did they manage to subdue this nation of proud warriors. **At a certain moment in the long sequence of Asante Wars, a group of Basel missionaries was captured in Anum, east of the Volta River. They were brought to the kingdom's capital, Kumase, and kept there during four years as hostages, albeit under a relatively mild regime of "town arrest"** (chapter 3.9.).

Given the political situation just mentioned, and also the arrangements made with other missionary organisations concerning their respective regional priorities, the Basel Mission was for the most part of the 19th century active in the inland area between the Volta and Pra Rivers.

Along the coast, the Basel people at first merely covered the Ga and Dangme speaking belt around Accra, later spreading to Winneba in the west and Ada in the east. Hence, the Basel Mission operated between the areas of the Bremen Mission which was engaged since 1847 in the core country of the Ewe, and that of the Wesleyan (Methodist) Mission, which had in 1835 established itself in Cape Coast and first tended to spread westward from there.

All of these mission societies had to stay clear of the Asante Kingdom, which then spread over the main parts of the forest belt. The only exception was a Wesleyan interlude in Kumase from 1840 to about 1870. During many of these years, however, its lone representative was not allowed to be active.

Only after the deportation of the incumbent Asantehene, Otumfuo Prempeh I, to Elmina Castle (and later to the Seychelles Islands, which marked the end of the Asante Wars) were Christian missions allowed into Asante. This became the high time for the Basel Mission, which methodically laid its network of mission stations over the realm.

Finally, the year 1918 brought an end to the involvement of the Basel Mission in Gold Coast as an independent church organisation.

At that time, the Mission was reaching out north as far as Yendi in the Savannah Belt, was approaching the border with the Ivory Coast in the western direction, and had consolidated its eastern positions along the Volta River. It thus had mission stations in an area covering about half of modern Ghana.[1]

Isn't That Amazing?

It is amazing to see the extent of missionary activities carried out by white people in West Africa. Almost two hundred years ago when there was no email, telephone, fax, jet airlines, electricity or running water, people were prepared to go as far as places like Yendi in the north of Ghana! Even today, in this 21st century, you would rarely find a Ghanaian pastor eager to go to Yendi.

Dear friend, the Europeans no longer believe in this Gospel which they died for. It is the turn of the people who still have faith, to take the Gospel to every remote corner.

May we go further than they did, because we have more knowledge, more revelation, more equipment and more access. May we cover more remote areas than they did! May we not fail in this God-given responsibility. We must win the lost at any cost! If we have to become missionaries, so be it! If we have to die in a foreign land, so be it!

"We would have considered it shameful to the name of Christ to close our hearts and ears to the misery and the outcries for help of these poor souls in Africa, just because we shied away from the dangers of death. Neither does the European slave trader shy away from the perils of a life-consuming climate, when he roams the same shores day and night like a predator..."

Inspector Blumhardt- 1826

CHAPTER 3

Keys to the Harvest

Why do pastors struggle and fight over sheep? Why do pastors want to have members from other churches in their church? Why do pastors start churches by breaking up other churches? I believe it is because they do not know the keys to the harvest. Let me share two important keys with you.

1.   The Key of Massive Organization

There are more than enough souls waiting to be saved. There are not enough buildings to contain the harvest if it were reaped. **Unlock the harvest with the key of massive organization. What do I mean by massive organization?** Pastors must mobilize their church members to have massive organized prayer, massive organized fasting and massive organized outreaches.

How utterly boring it must be if a Christian's life is just listening to a thirty-minute sermon every week. For goodness sake, there must be more to Christianity than being a pew-warmer. Christians will find satisfaction when they fast and pray for souls.

Do you know why many people do not attend prayer meetings? It is because the pastor himself does not get involved.

Fasting and prayer is the key that removes scales from a sinner's eyes. When you pray before witnessing, you will have better results. People will be saved! Just like Jesus, you will be anointed when you pray. If you are not prayerful, people will just tell you, "I see your point, but I don't agree with you." All your preaching will be like water dripping off a duck's back!

I'm speaking to pastors now! Mobilize the entire church to pray. Mobilize the entire church to fast. Pray for church growth. Pray for salvation. Pray for people to become born again. You will have tremendous results.

A pastor's job is not just to preach and teach, but to lead the sheep. You must lead the sheep into outreaches and soul winning. They will be blessed when they have something to do with their spiritual energy.

Organize crusades, breakfast meetings, door-to-door witnessing, street evangelism and concerts that win souls. Involve the whole church and discover the joy of soul winning.

On one of the Sundays, send out your members to bring in anyone they can find on the streets. The following week, organize "Operation Bring-Your-Family" - that is, a Sunday when everyone brings his or her household to church. Then plan for Sundays when you can have "Operation Bring-Your-Colleagues". The whole church will invite their co-workers to church. You will experience tremendous church growth.

One day, find out how many members of your church were saved in the church. As you do more soul winning, you will find out that more and more of your members will come in through soul winning.

It is better to have church growth through soul winning than through the transfer of angry and discontented members from other churches.

2. The Key of Anagkazo

"Anagkazo" is a Greek word which means "to compel, to force, to drive, to necessitate, to threaten and to use any means at your disposal" to convince someone (Luke 14:23). You will discover that Jesus used the word *"anagkazo"* when he was speaking about evangelism. The master sent out his servants to *anagkazo* anyone they could find on the streets, highways, hedges and in the gutters.

And the lord said unto the servant, Go out into the highways and hedges, and compel [*anagkazo*] them to come in, that my house may be filled.

Luke 14:23

Many of those originally invited to the party did not bother to come. What is Jesus trying to tell us? **The Lord is showing us that gentle invitations will not reach the lost.** We have to use any other means at our disposal. Our churches will be empty if we do not use the key of *anagkazo.*

Earlier in this book, I spoke of how we organized an international crusade at a prominent park in our city. Many souls were saved during those three days. One of the keys that we used was *the key of anagkazo.* When the crowd had gathered, we gave a command to the old and young alike. We told them to go out into the streets where the prostitutes and broken-hearted were and bring them in. There was a clear command, "Do not return to the crusade alone. You must bring a soul with you!"

I went out myself with the visiting American evangelist, and together we brought back some people to the crusade grounds. We are not trying to impress anybody. We are trying to obey our Master's command. Many things that are impressive to man are not impressive to God.

I heard one evangelist describing how he had printed several million books and had them distributed to every home in a part of Europe. I was most excited when he said that seventy thousand people had written back responding to Christ through the books.

That is *anagkazo* at work - forcing the Gospel into every home! He was using every means available to push the Gospel into rebellious European letter boxes.

Dear friends, our gentle Christian smiles have little effect in a hostile world filled with sceptical people. People do not trust anything or anyone! Africans thought they could trust their leaders. Then came African dictators, who like vampires, sucked the wealth of their nations. Americans thought they could trust their president and then came the presidential scandals.

People thought they could trust the engineers and pilots and then came the TWA, Swissair, Kenya Airways and the Concorde crashes. Many people trusted pastors and then came the tele-evangelists' scandals.

Folks are sceptical about the solutions we offer through Christ. It is time for us to rise up with the key of *anagkazo* and bring in the harvest. Let us use every means available, such as invitations, entreaties and warnings. Let us use the radio, television and the print media. Let's go out there to a dying world and give them the good news of salvation.

If someone's house was on fire and you could see that he was about to perish, would you give him a gentle nudge or would you shake him out of his sleep? Win the lost at any cost! Win the lost if it means using *anagkazo*. *(See the book "Anagkazo" by this author.)*

CHAPTER 4

The Follow-Up Ministry

Population/Follow-Up Graph

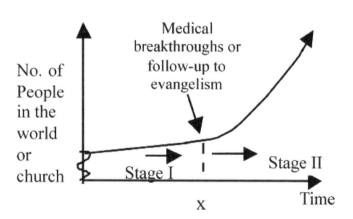

Stage I

- Mortality rate was high.

- No medicines, no medical answers.

- The growth of the population was very slow.

Stage II

- At time "x" there was a medical revolution.

- Mortality rate was greatly reduced: fewer people were dying.

- Suddenly, the population began to shoot up rapidly.

If a church is at Stage I there is little or no growth. *When a church begins to practise follow-up, it retains the converts it gets from evangelism. Notice how the growth of the church increases in Stage II.*

You will notice from the graph that follow-up leads to retention of souls. **Without a follow-up ministry, evangelism is virtually a waste of time, money and resources.** All our efforts will be in vain. Every church must develop an effective follow-up ministry that deals with the souls that come to the Lord.

Don't Abandon Your New Baby

The follow-up ministry is a scientific way of preventing the loss of converts. So much energy is spent in winning the lost. A proportional amount of time and resources must be spent to retain the harvest. One of the saddest things I saw in the hospital, was a little baby that had been abandoned by its mother. The mother had gone through nine months of pregnancy, struggled in the labour ward and finally delivered a bouncing baby girl.

When no one was watching, this lady slipped out of the labour ward and vanished. What was going to happen to that baby? Her future lay in the hands of fate. I felt particularly sorry when the nurses had to ask some of the lactating mothers to donate some milk to the baby.

Let me also ask this: What is going to happen to all the souls who come to the Lord? **Follow-up is to new converts as breastfeeding is to babies.**

The growth of the population of the world is very similar to the growth of the church. The population of the world had been considerably low for hundreds of years. At the turn of the century, things began to change and the population began to increase dramatically.

The reason for this turning point was not because people were having more babies. Neither was it due to younger people having more children. It was due to the improvement in medical science that occurred at the beginning of the twentieth century. A drastic reduction in the mortality rate has resulted in a much larger population.

If the church were to do follow-up, and retain the people we won, the church would experience major growth. Planting churches where crusades and evangelism have taken place is another major part of follow-up. Follow-up also involves prayer for the converts that have been won to the Lord.

> **My little children, of whom I TRAVAIL [pray] in birth again until Christ be formed in you.**
>
> **Galatians 4:19**

You must travail for your souls in prayer. That is how to follow them up spiritually. After spiritual follow-up, you must visit them. New converts are established through visitation. In my church, we do not only have counsellors but we have people who go to the homes of the converts as well.

Avoid This Mistake

One common mistake people make when they do follow-up is to waste time on non-serious and "un-saved" converts. Paul told Timothy to spend time on faithful people who were serious about Christ.

And the things that thou hast heard of me among many witnesses, the same commit thou to faithful men, who shall be able to teach others also.

2 Timothy 2:2

CHAPTER 5

Letters of a Soul Winner

As far back as I can remember, I have always had a vision to win souls for Christ. During my early days at the university, I met a law student called E.A.T. Sackey. He happened to be a classmate and a friend of my wife, so naturally we became good friends. I soon discovered that he and I had similar interests like soul winning. I believe that is what drew us together in ministry.

I recently discovered some of the letters he wrote to me when we were both students in the university in 1988. At the time, I was a medical student and he was a law student, but neither medicine nor law could drown our divine call and desire to win more people to Christ. I am glad that we are both in the ministry today.

I feel very happy when I see the lost being preached to. I am reproducing below, four letters my friend wrote to me. As you read them, I believe you will be inspired to launch out into the harvest.

Four Memorable Letters

1. **A Baptism of Zeal**

2. **Dreaming about Evangelism**

3. **I'm With You**

4. **Let's Die Preaching**

A Baptism of Zeal

29-5-1986

Dag,

If ever we need a baptism from heaven, it should be a baptism of zeal. "The zeal of thine house has consumed me." We really need to be eaten up dry with a passionate passion.

A burden that would make us uncomfortable until we see and get men saved from the blackness of darkness into the kingdom of His dear Son. *This should be our waking thoughts and sleeping dreams.*

We really need the love that is blind to all the possible dangers of the mission. Love that ignores personal safety, disregards the odds against it, drops "sacrifice" from its vocabulary, requires no crutches, ignores all dangers and is intolerant to idleness.

Remember that the master went out at the ELEVENTH HOUR and He found some men still IDLING in the market places. May God help us!

In this eleventh hour, the church seems to be idling, careless of its responsibilities. I'm really doubtful whether I'll want to be part of this system. I'm beginning to believe that it is not the sin of the world that is making the Church sick, but rather the sin and unconcern of the Church that is making the world sick. I'm getting fed up with complacency in the church. I'm filled with Holy anger - against the devil, against sin, against our unbelief AND also against the Church.

Everything in the world is broken - confidence in government, confidence in the dollar, marriages are breaking up and teenagers are breaking up their minds with drugs. All is broken - except one thing, the hearts of the believers. But I believe that we need broken hearts to face this colossal mess. Weeping is a command. But there should be action after that (Joel 2:7).

The present lethargy in the Church is almost unpardonable. I need to bear a broken heart over the coldness in the church. Yay!! The fields are really white.

DAG, LETS BIND OUR HEARTS TO THE REACHING OF THE UNREACHED. *We need to become impervious to the opinions of others about our zeal. We should not care what it would cost us to be burnt out for God. Whether we are flattered or fattened, esteemed or despised, condemned a fool or a philosopher, through evil report or good report, kisses or curses, we should be set to do the will of Him who sent us.*

We need to move out and away from the centralised system we seem to be having in Accra. The Church is founded with showmanship, competition, "holding the form of religion but denying the power thereof" (2 Timothy 3:5).

Although the Pharisee's prayer is always seen as not good enough - ("God I thank Thee I am not like other people: swindlers, unjust, adulterers, etc."), how many church folks can pray such prayers anyway? May God help us!

I pray, like Habakkuk did, "LORD, IN YOUR WRATH, REMEMBER MERCY."

Love to all.

EATS

Co-Worker

Dreaming about Evangelism

c/o C 52

An/Sarbah Hall

1987

Hi Brother Dag,

"I thank my God upon every remembrance of you." Well, since you have so much to do in these crucial times, I had better write just a note, and not a letter.

I always thank God for the mission God has called us to. Yesterday God told me clearly that I had better get serious with this ministry because the time is short, and I know you agree as well. Dag, I am bent on seeing the mighty hand of God in our ministry.

I'll never be satisfied with anything short of that, and God Himself knows. As we launch out, I'm so certain of the fact that God will be confirmed, so that what was said of Christ, *"that a man approved of God by many signs and wonders"* would also be said of us and the ministry; so that man's faith will not rely on the wisdom of men but the power of God.

I know that we really do a lot. I see you as an answer to a need in my life. You might not understand this very well, but I hope Maame would explain it further. THE HOLD OF EVANGELISM ON ME GETS STRONGER WITH EVERY PASSING DAY. IT NEVER LESSENS. I DREAM OF IT, WAKE UP WITH THAT DREAM AND GO TO BED, WITH IT STILL OCCUPYING THE GREATER PART OF MY MIND.

I know that God will lead us by His own Spirit and we shall see with our own eyes utterly, many coming to taste for the first time *"the unspeakable gift."* Whatever the Holy Spirit tells you and whatever leading He gives you, be sure that I'll agree with you.

Dag, we have to make it, we can make it, and we will make it in Jesus' name.

Well, for the sake of formality let me just wish you success in your exams. You're a stranger to failure.

Regards to Asamoah, Stanley, Donkash and all those who call on the Lord from a pure heart. Grace and peace be multiplied unto you.

I planned coming to church there on Sunday but I can't because I'm supposed to preach at Nautical College. I'll be there the next Sunday.

Love from Cynthia, of course.

Affections,

Brother T

I hope that after exams you'll be free enough with the permission of M so that we can talk and pray for these times.

I'm with You

Pastor,

I thank my God upon every remembrance of you. In fact, you mean so much to me, and I don't feel worthy to be a co-worker with you. However, God has considered my low estate and given me favour in your sight. Henceforth all men shall call me blessed!! Please don't let Maame tell you that these are my usual and normal raps. I mean this with all my heart and God is my witness.

Well Pastor, I have great confidence in you as my Pastor and I know we are a terror to the kingdom of the devil and a great embarrassment to demons. Hallelujah.

We're going to work together, walk together and be an unflinching threat to the negative spiritual world.

And I also wish to use this occasion to reaffirm my pledge and commitment to you. I want you to know that, you can trust me to the last degree. I'm very stable and settled in mind, purpose, and objective.

Glory to Jesus!!

I really wish I could come home and give you a birthday hug, but where I am, I'm restrained and inhibited by our perceiving circumstances. I'm with you in the spirit any way.

Bro. T

Let's Die Preaching

C47 An/Sarbah

Legon

20/6/86

Hello Brother Dag,

Only the Holy Ghost can reveal to you what's been going on in my heart since I came from Korle-Bu. Like I said, I never knew that you had such a vision at all. I really bless God for you and for making us to know each other in these times when so many believers are seeing the 2nd coming of Christ and the end of the age as only subjects for rare curiosity.

*The hope of Christ's return is certainly not an escapist clause. **It's not an alibi for non-involvement. To the contrary, it's a spur to holiness, to evangelism and to obedience.** It's a maturation to make God's words on earth OUR OWN, for as Jesus said, "Occupy till I come" (Luke 19:13).*

One man said we are to behave and give and love and work as though Jesus Christ died yesterday, rose today and is coming again tomorrow.

Surely, the greatest need of the Church today is not more members, more buildings, more money. The supreme issue is missions and evangelism, repentance and revival. It is not great strength or great wealth that Christ calls for in His Church on the eve of His coming. It is great faithfulness to Him and great obedience to His will and to the opportunities He gives us.

DAG, LET'S DIE PREACHING! *Let's give our whole heart to it. Let's make it our own business so that we can say with Paul, "My Gospel". It makes a lot of difference.*

Let's be pliable tools in the hands of the Master. He really needs us. I'm dying to see next term come. Our, at long last, sign-wonder-miracle which we have desired is near us!! Glory.

I can see my own come to know God, I can see the power of God present to lead, and to see establishment and abundance in the kingdom of God. Glory!!

Dag, I'm quite sorry if I've not been able to express myself quite well. The Spirit will reveal it to you. I have a burden I cannot describe. It keeps bubbling in my heart and belly. The Word of God is like fire in my bones. Oh, the world is waiting for us.

There's a command from above: "Go ye unto all the world". There's a cry from beneath: "Father Abraham send somebody to preach to my relatives," and there's a call from without "Come over to Macedonia and help us".

WE SHALL SURELY DO IT, IF EVEN IT MEANS SACRIFICING AND INVESTING OUR LAST PENNY INTO IT, OR EVEN WALKING OVER BROKEN BOTTLES.

And the God of All Grace shall see us through. Regards from my beloved C.

EATS

CHAPTER 6

A Prayer and a Prophecy

Lord Jesus, I pray for your people. I pray with all my heart for everyone who reads this book.

I pray that you will transmit into their hearts the burden that You have Oh Lord. Show them the reason why You created the Church - the reason why we exist. And the reason why You brought us together as a Church. Show us Oh Lord the reason why we gather each time.

Help us to know that it is not to show off our new dresses, our new suits and our new shoes. Show us I pray, Oh Lord! Reveal it to each person who reads this book. I cannot explain it to them, Lord. I have done my best. I have spoken and I have written, but it is you, Holy Spirit, who can reveal it to the people.

Lord, reveal yourself. Select the evangelists you are looking for. Find the people you are searching for to help you accomplish this great work! I see a vast harvest before us. I pray Oh God that the burden will come upon your people. I pray for the financiers, that you will anoint them and give them the hearts of soul winners.

I pray for the supporters and the helpers who help us in the ministry. They are people who assist us to do your Great Commission. Oh God, I am praying for them today.

Holy Spirit, open the eyes of your people and let us see the harvest that is ripe and waiting for us. Help us to notice the lost, walking aimlessly around us. Let us see how people are wandering about as sheep without a shepherd.

Jesus, I pray that you will walk in the midst of your people and touch our eyes and hearts again. Let us know why we are alive! Reveal to us what we are supposed to be doing. Oh Lord Jesus, I pray with all my heart. I cannot show them, but you can. Holy Spirit, you can show your people what you want.

Lord, I cannot transmit it to them but you can. Father, in the name of Jesus, let your work be done and let your kingdom come. Let your work be more important to us than anything else. Let souls begin to be harvested. Let the finances come in to support this great effort. Give us a heart, Heavenly Father, for souls. Help us to win the lost at any cost.

Give the pastors a heart for soul winning. As we shepherd your sheep, let us never forget why we are shepherds. Help us to be more like you who came to seek and to save that which was lost. I pray in the name of Jesus. Thank you LORD. AMEN!

A PROPHECY

Today, certain people are stars in this world. O Lord you have shown us clearly that in the days to come, different people are going to be stars. They that win souls and they that turn many to righteousness shall shine as the stars forever.

They are going to be the people that know their God. The stars are going to be people that have turned many to righteousness. Yea, they shall be those who have contributed to the winning and reaping of souls to the kingdom of God. They shall be those who have brought in the harvest, saith, the Spirit of the Lord.

This is my commission to the church. This is the great commission to the church and the people of God. This is the work that I have called you to do. To go out there and win them. Say not, "It is not yet time." Say not, "I will do it next year." For the fields are white and the harvest is ready. For the people are waiting in their great numbers to be harvested and to be won to me. Yea, Islam is not the way, the truth and the life. No one, no one cometh unto the Father but by me. Therefore, take this message to the world.

Take the Word of God, which is like a hammer, saith the Lord. Take the Word of God, which is like a fire, and go forth with that fire. Go forth with the hammer. Go forth in the power of my Word. For my Word shall go and shall not return unto me void but it shall accomplish those things which it has been sent to do, saith the Spirit of God.

Listen to me, the stars are going to change. They are going to change. The Lord is saying that there is something in it for you. There is a future for you.

Do not be short-sighted. Do not see only today, but see the years ahead. See eternity! You can shine like a star in eternity.

[77]Eternity will begin, it will begin shortly. It will begin soon, saith the Spirit.

THE END!